ScriptureWalk Senior High Discipleship

ScriptureWalk Senior High Discipleship

Bible-Based Sessions for Teens

Nora Bradbury-Haehl

Saint Mary's Press
Christian Brothers Publications
Winona, Minnesota

Genuine recycled paper with 10% post-consumer waste.
Printed with soy-based ink.

Thank you to the teenagers at Saint Joseph's Parish, Penfield, New York, and Holy Trinity Parish, Webster, New York, especially the youth leaders and GROOP staff.

The publishing team included Brian Singer-Towns, development editor; Mary Duerson, copy editor; Barbara Bartelson, production editor; Hollace Storkel, typesetter; Cindi Ramm, art director; Alicia María Sánchez and Cären Yang, cover designers; produced by the graphics division of Saint Mary's Press.

The scriptural quotations contained herein are from the New Revised Standard Version of the Bible. Copyright © 1989 by the Division of Christian Education of the National Council of the Churches of Christ in the United States of America. All rights reserved.
    The article in appendix A is reprinted from the *Catholic Herald,* 16 December 1999.
    The illustration on page 16 is by Tim Foley.
    The illustrations on pages 24, 42, 59, and 69 and the Study It and Live It icons used throughout the book were created by Sam Thiewes.
    The illustrations on pages 33, 50, and 78 are by Michael O. McGrath.
    The Pray It icon used throughout the book is from Click Art software.
    The cover photo is by CORBIS, Darrell Gulin.

Copyright © 2000 by Saint Mary's Press, 702 Terrace Heights, Winona MN 55987-1320. All rights reserved. Permission is granted to reproduce only the materials intended for distribution to the program participants. No other part of this book may be reproduced by any means without the written permission of the publisher.

Printed in the United States of America

Printing: 9 8 7 6 5 4 3 2 1

Year: 2008 07 06 05 04 03 02 01 00

ISBN 0-88489-642-0

To my mom, who helped me see things from the other point of view, and my dad, who asked, "What would Jesus do?"

Contents

Introduction 8

Session 1   **Death**
John 11:1–44 16

Study It: Roll Away the Stone 17
Live It: Ripples 20
Pray It: Seeds of New Life 22

Session 2   **Discipleship**
Luke 9:1–6 24

Study It: Disciple Do's and Don'ts 25
Live It: Following in Jesus' Footsteps 28
Pray It: Lord, Bless Our Feet 30

Session 3   **Fear**
Psalm 91 33

Study It: Fear Versus Trust 34
Live It: Naming Our Monsters 37
Pray It: Releasing Our Fears 39

Session 4   **Finding Happiness**
Luke 12:4–34 42

Study It: Finding True Happiness 43
Live It: Where Is Your Treasure? 46
Pray It: Leaving Your Burdens Behind 48

Session 5	**Prayer**	
	Matthew 6:5–15 50	
	Study It: What Do You Pray For? 51	
	Live It: Prayer Sticks 54	
	Pray It: God-the-Good-Parent Reflection 56	
Session 6	**Sadness and Depression**	
	Job 7:1–11 59	
	Study It: Acknowledging Our Sadness 60	
	Live It: Recipes to Cure the Blues 63	
	Pray It: A Litany of Healing 66	
Session 7	**Sexuality**	
	Song of Solomon 2:1–17 69	
	Study It: Sexuality—God's Gift 70	
	Live It: Sexuality Pinwheels 73	
	Pray It: God's Love Song 76	
Session 8	**Witnessing Your Faith**	
	John 4:1–42 78	
	Study It: Witnessing Your Faith 79	
	Live It: Telling Your Story 82	
	Pray It: Living Water Reflection 84	
Appendix A	Reading the Scriptures as a Catholic 89	
Appendix B	ScriptureWalk Bookmarks 91	

Introduction

The Reason for the ScriptureWalk Series

The search for both meaning and mystery is a powerful quest with young people, especially as they begin to form their own personal worldview during adolescence. As young people journey through this stage of life, they begin to ask important spiritual questions, such as How did life start? Why do bad things happen to good or innocent people? What is my purpose? Where is God? and even, Is God?

In the search for answers to these questions, the Bible shines like a beacon. Within the Bible's pages, God's word sheds light on both the meaning and the mystery of life. The more young people are assisted in reading and reflecting on the powerful messages contained in the Scriptures, the better equipped they will be for the spiritual journey, both individually and communally.

Vatican Council II opened the doors for Catholics to read and study the Bible with renewed fervor. In the last few decades, parish Scripture study groups have sprung up across the country as Catholic adults began to enthusiastically explore the Bible. However, the Catholic scriptural renewal has yet to fully flower among Catholic young people, partly owing to a lack of resources designed to engage Catholic young people in Bible study and reflection. The ScriptureWalk series is designed to help fill that gap.

Bringing the Scriptures to Life

God speaks to us through the Bible whomever we are and wherever we are and whatever age we might be. The Bible is a source of strength and a source of challenge. The Scriptures have an incredible power to transform our life. If we invite the Scriptures off the written page and into our life and heart, we cannot help but be changed in a radical way. *The ScriptureWalk Senior High* sessions in this book will help you in making the Bible come alive for your senior high youth.

The Goals of *ScriptureWalk Senior High: Discipleship*

ScriptureWalk Senior High: Discipleship has four goals:
- That the young people study the Bible using a group process that is consistent with Catholic scriptural interpretation
- That the young people apply the Bible's teachings to their life as young disciples

Introduction

- That volunteer youth or adult leaders use the session components in a variety of settings
- That the young people are motivated to read and reflect on the Scriptures as a part of their regular prayer life

In addressing these goals, this volume of the ScriptureWalk series contains eight sessions on topics connected to discipleship. Empowering young people to live as disciples of Jesus Christ is an important priority for Catholic youth ministry. It is a named goal in *Renewing the Vision: A Framework for Catholic Youth Ministry* (Washington, D.C.: United States Catholic Conference, 1997). The discipleship themes in these sessions were chosen based on a survey of Catholic youth leaders. The Bible passages used with each theme were carefully selected to speak authentically to the topic.

The Structure of *ScriptureWalk Senior High*

All the *ScriptureWalk Senior High* books give group leaders a great deal of flexibility in how they use the session components. Each session is divided into three separate but interrelated components. These components can be used together to create a 90-minute session on a particular theme, they can be used separately to enhance other events, or they can be combined in various ways to create new activities. To facilitate this independent use, each of the three components starts on a new page and has its own list of needed materials, unless no special materials are required. When appropriate, special instructions are included for using a component as an independent activity. Each component is also designated by a special icon. The icon appears at the top of every page containing directions for that component. This will help in locating directions for a specific component. The icons with descriptions of the three components follow.

Study It

The first component of every session in this book is called Study It and takes 45 to 60 minutes. The Study It component is essentially a five-step Bible study process on the session theme. The steps are described more fully in this introduction, in the section titled "Leading the Study It Component."

Live It

The second component of each session is called Live It. It consists of a 15- to 30-minute activity engaging the young people in the session topic in an active and thought-provoking way. The Live It component can lead them to better understand how the Bible's teaching on the topic can be lived out today.

In addition to the primary activity, I have included an alternative approach for the Live It component. It gives you an option to consider using with your group. Like the primary activity, it engages the young people in a fun and active way, but it is described in less detail. After you have looked over the primary activity, consider the potential of the alternative approach for fitting your group's interest.

9

Introduction

 **Pray It**

The third component of each session is Pray It, a 10- to 15-minute prayer service on the theme of the session's Scripture passage. The prayer services use guided meditation, shared prayer, music, silence, and reflective readings. The Pray It component gives the young people an opportunity to bring their insights and concerns to God in prayer.

Suggestions for Program Leaders

Where and When Should I Use These Sessions?

The active-learning techniques and small-group discussions of *ScriptureWalk Senior High* sessions make them ideal for use with either high school youth groups or catechetical programs. The sessions are arranged alphabetically by topic. They do not build on one another, so you can use them independently whenever your group wants (or needs!) to study a particular topic. Or you can use all eight sessions as a semester course on life issues. You can create 60- to 90-minute (or even longer) sessions by using one, two, or three of the components.

Keep in mind that each of the three session components can be used independently. This allows for great flexibility in how you use them. For example, a group of young people meeting after school for an hour-long Bible study might use only the Study It and Pray It portions of a session. Or a parish youth ministry coordinator might choose to use all three components of a session as one integrated activity during a retreat. In still another setting, a leader might decide to use the Pray It component from the discipleship session to conclude a youth group meeting on discipleship.

Consider how you might use the *ScriptureWalk Senior High* components in the following settings:
- Catholic high school religion classes
- youth group meetings
- retreats
- parish religious education classes
- Confirmation preparation classes
- leadership training sessions
- mentor programs
- intergenerational activities

What Group Size Works with These Sessions?

The time estimates for the session components are based on a group size of ten to fifteen young people. However, by slightly adjusting the session plans, they can be used with groups as small as five or as large as sixty. For example, when doing a discussion exercise with a large group, invite only a limited number of participants to share their thoughts. Or break the large group into smaller groups. Look over the session plan in advance to determine which activities will work better with a large group and which will work better with small groups.

For discussions in the Study It components, it is important to work in groups of five to eight young people, thus allowing everyone more opportunity to share their thoughts on the Bible passage and the discussion questions. If you are doing several topics from *Scripture-Walk Senior High* with the same large group, you may want to keep the small discussion groups consistent from session to session to encourage deeper sharing over time.

What Bible Should I Use?

Ideally, every person participating in *ScriptureWalk Senior High* will have his or her own Bible to use. This can help the participants become more comfortable in using the Bible. Use a Catholic edition containing both the Old and New Testaments. Avoid translations that use archaic language (like the King James version) or paraphrasing (like the Living Bible). The New American Bible and the Catholic edition of the New Revised Standard Version are good choices.

We strongly recommend using a youth-friendly study Bible such as *The Catholic Youth Bible,* published by Saint Mary's Press. Such Bibles commonly contain helpful background articles and introductions to individual books of the Bible that can enrich the participants' knowledge and discussion.

Leading the Study It Component

The Study It component is the heart of each *ScriptureWalk Senior High* session. It has a consistent five-step format. The steps are explained below with suggestions for leading each one.

Step 1: Opening activity
Each session starts with a catchy, short activity introducing the participants to the session theme. The activities are simple and take 10 minutes or less. If your group is large, the opening activity could be done as a large group. Or you could break the group into small groups of five to eight before the opening activity and have the young people stay in their group for the whole Bible study. You can designate a young person in each group as its facilitator. Or you may wish to have young adult or adult facilitators.

Step 2: Proclamation
In this step the Scripture passage chosen to address the session topic is proclaimed. Proclaiming the Scriptures is different from simply reading them. Proclamation implies an intentional reading, done with feeling and conviction. You may proclaim the reading yourself, or you may ask a participant to do it. If you have a large group that has already divided into small groups, assign and prepare a reader for each group. Give the person or persons proclaiming the passage some time to practice. Be sure the person proclaiming the passage in each group does not disturb the other groups by reading too loudly.

Have group members follow along in their Bible while the passage is being read. Although reading along in this way would not be appropriate in a eucharistic liturgy, it is appropriate and even desirable for a Bible study.

Introduction

Step 3: Initial reaction

In this step the young people briefly react to the Scripture passage they have just heard. Believers are convinced that God does speak to us through the Bible. An age-old practice for helping us listen to what God is saying is to listen for words, phrases, or stories that strike a chord within us. Three or four reflection questions in this step help the young people do that. Emphasize that the questions have no right or wrong answers. And do not try to force the discussion of them to go on too long. Usually, 5 to 10 minutes suffice.

If your group is large and you have not already divided it into small groups, do so for this step. Each discussion group may have five to eight people. The young people will work in these small groups for this discussion and the final discussion in step 5.

Step 4: Commentary

After the initial reaction to the Scripture passage, the leader presents a brief commentary on the passage. The commentary gives background on the passage's historical situation and the church's interpretation of it. This sets the stage for the application step, in which the young people apply the passage to their life today. The commentary helps them make this application in light of the church's understanding of the passage, rather than entirely based on their personal interpretation.

You can deliver the commentary in several ways:
- Read it out loud to the group as it is written.
- Photocopy it and give a copy to each participant to read over silently, or ask one person to read it out loud while the others follow along.
- Present it in your own words. Write the major points out on newsprint to add emphasis.
- If you have formed small discussion groups, designate a reader in each group and give her or him a copy of it to read aloud.

Regardless of the method employed, this step should be short and simple, no more than 5 minutes.

Step 5: Application

The final step is a sharing exercise in which the group's initial reaction and the commentary are connected to the experience of young people today. Depending on how comfortable the participants are with one another, and on how talkative they tend to be, this step can last 15 to 25 minutes. Allow enough time for the young people to really grapple with the implications of the biblical message.

Given your knowledge of the young people in your group, before the session, review the discussion questions in this step and decide which ones to ask and which ones to drop. Rephrase or add questions if you think doing so might spark discussion better.

Challenge each participant to search for her or his personal answers to the reflection questions. Do not allow a few participants to dominate the discussion. One good strategy for involving everyone is to first ask the participants to journal or reflect quietly on a question or set of questions for a couple of minutes. Then invite them to share their reflections out loud. This allows the more introverted members time to formulate their responses and encourages the extroverted members to think more deeply about their answers.

Introduction

Prepare, Prepare, Prepare!

Prepare for a session by reading over its components and deciding which ones to use. Become familiar with the commentary in the Study It component. If necessary, look up additional background in a Bible commentary or a Bible dictionary (see the resources at the end of this introduction). Be sure to gather the necessary supplies and take care of any other preparations. To help you with this, when appropriate, each component begins with a materials needed list and a list of other necessary preparations. Be sure to look at these lists for each component that you are using.

Put Together a Supply Box

Many of the same materials are needed for each session. You can save time by collecting these materials in a supply box and having it on hand for each session. We recommend that the box include the following items:
- Bibles, one for each person
- pens or pencils
- markers
- scrap paper
- newsprint
- several pairs of scissors
- a candle and matches
- a tape or CD player, and recordings of reflective instrumental music
- masking tape
- a Bible concordance
- a Bible commentary

Involve the Participants

When conducting *ScriptureWalk Senior High* sessions or activities, use young people in leadership roles as much as possible. One of the best ways to learn about something is to teach it to others. So as you prepare for a session, consider ways participants can be invited to lead parts of each component. You might ask them to proclaim a reading, lead a prayer experience, or conduct a group discussion. Any of the session readings or directions can be photocopied for this purpose. When group members are involved, they are more likely to learn and grow.

Adapt the Components to Fit Your Group

Like individuals, each group is unique. To use a session exactly as it is written may not be the most effective strategy for your group. While preparing for the session, think of the unique traits of your group members. Which session questions, activities, or prayers seem to speak to them and their life situations? Which do not? Can the latter be altered or adjusted to make them relevant? Often, slightly changing the wording of a question or adding a step to an activity can make the difference between a successful group experience and an incredibly successful group experience!

Introduction

Set Up an Appealing Environment

Even the most prepared group leader will have a difficult time getting the group members involved if the meeting environment is uncomfortable, uninviting, or distracting. Take time to evaluate your physical environment:
- Provide sufficient light. The room should be neither too bright nor too dark.
- Avoid areas with continual distractions: doors being opened and closed, phones ringing, or people walking by.
- Consider having snacks and beverages available for participants before the session or during a break.
- Arrange the chairs for small groups in a circle to reflect the idea that everyone in the group is on equal ground.

Also notice the relational environment. Make the participants feel welcome. Actions like the following can make a big difference:
- Warmly greet the participants by name.
- Help group members learn and use one another's names throughout the session.
- As new people enter the group, invite the current members to welcome and orient them.

Session Follow-Up Ideas

ScriptureWalk Senior High provides two tools to help the young people continue their reflection after the session, either individually or with their family. The first tool is a short section at the end of each session called Family Connection. This section gives a simple, family-based follow-up idea for the session. You may wish to send the ideas home in a newsletter, photocopy them for the participants, or simply suggest them to the young people at the end of the session.

The second tool is a bookmark containing five Scripture passages and related questions for individuals to use for reflection or journaling after each session. A different bookmark has been created specifically for each session. They are grouped together in appendix B of this manual. Photocopy the bookmarks for your group. Note that many of the Scripture passages on the bookmarks are also connected to informative articles in *The Catholic Youth Bible,* published by Saint Mary's Press.

Interpreting the Scriptures

Contextualism Versus Fundamentalism

ScriptureWalk Senior High uses a contextualist approach to interpreting the Scriptures. Contextualism is one of two very different approaches that Christians take in interpreting the Scriptures. The other approach, often referred to as fundamentalism, views all the stories and information in the Bible as historical and scientific fact. For example, a fundamentalist approach insists that God did in fact create the world in six 24-hour days.

Like the fundamentalist approach, the contextualist approach believes the Bible is true and without error in teaching the things God wants us to know for our salvation. But the contextualist approach does not insist that all the stories and information in the Bible must be interpreted as historical and scientific fact. A contextualist approach keeps in mind the literary genre or style of a particular book, the cultural background of the inspired author's original audience, and the church's ongoing teaching about the particular passage. For example, someone approaching the creation stories with a contextualist approach would recognize that the inspired author was using a mythic type of literature to teach that God is creator of all that is and that human beings have a responsibility toward God, creation, and other people. Given the literary genre, someone using this approach would not look for a scientific explanation in the story of how the world was created.

The Catholic church embraces and teaches the contextualist approach to the Scriptures, and, as mentioned above, it is used in *ScriptureWalk Senior High*. This approach to reading and interpreting the Scriptures requires more of the reader than does taking the stories literally, word for word, but it leads to more accurate and faithful interpretation. For more background on the Catholic understanding of the Bible, see the article in appendix A, "Reading the Scriptures as a Catholic."

Suggested Resources

An overwhelming number of resources for studying the Bible are available. The following resources are recommended for leaders and groups using *ScriptureWalk Senior High:*

Achtemeier, Paul J., gen. ed. *HarperCollins Bible Dictionary.* [SanFrancisco]: HarperSanFrancisco, 1996. Provides helpful information on people, places, and concepts in the Bible.

Bergant, Dianne, and Robert J. Karris, gen. eds. *Collegeville Bible Commentary.* Collegeville, MN: Liturgical Press, 1989. Gives detailed information and interpretation for each book in the Bible.

The Bible Library for Catholics. Liguori Software, 800-325-9521. This computer CD-ROM has three complete Catholic translations of the Bible, Nave's Topical Index, search software, and more.

Kohlenberger, John R., III, ed. *The Concise Concordance to the New Revised Standard Version.* New York: Oxford University Press, 1993. Bible concordances show all the places selected words and themes can be found in a particular version of the Bible.

Ralph, Margaret Nutting. *"And God Said What?" An Introduction to Biblical Literary Forms for Bible Lovers.* New York: Paulist Press, 1986. A wonderful introduction to interpreting the Bible from a contextualist approach.

Singer-Towns, Brian. *The Bible: Power and Promise.* Winona, MN: Saint Mary's Press, 1997. This course from the Horizons series contains five sessions introducing the Bible to senior high students. You may wish to use some or all of the course with your group before using *ScriptureWalk Senior High.*

Session 1

Death

John 11:1–44

For Christians the central mystery of our faith revolves around death and resurrection. This session focuses on the raising of Lazarus. The story of Lazarus is a promise that offers young people a new perspective on death. It reveals not only the grief and loss that accompany death but also the hope that comes from knowing Christ's triumph over death. This story can help young people understand that for Christians death is an experience of both grief and hope.

Death

 **Study It**

Roll Away the Stone (45–60 minutes)

Materials Needed
- ☐ Bibles, one for each person
- ☐ fine-tip markers, one for each person
- ☐ a basket of small stones, at least one stone for each person

Before the Session
- ☐ If you plan to have a student proclaim the Scriptures in step 2, tell him or her ahead of time so that he or she can practice.
- ☐ Decide how you will present the commentary in step 4 (see page 12 of the introduction for options).

Step 1 — **Opening Activity (10 minutes)**

Explain to the young people that this session is about death, our responses to it, and what our Christian faith tells us about it. Give everyone a fine-tip marker and invite them each to choose a stone from a basket of small stones. Tell them to imagine that in sixty or seventy years, their little stone will be their headstone and that because the stone is so small, they will be allowed just one word on it as a memorial of their life. Invite the participants to think about their life. Ask: "At the end of your life, how do you hope to be remembered? What one word will you write on this stone?" If the group is slow in starting, offer the following suggestions: loving, successful, forgiving, wife, husband, grandpa, grandma, faithful, generous, caring, strong, joyful.

Give everyone a little time to think and to write their word on their stone. Then invite them to share their word with the group if they wish. It is more important that everyone be given a chance to consider the question than to have everyone answer out loud.

Step 2 — **Proclamation (5-10 minutes)**

Direct the young people to open their Bible to John 11:1–44 so that they can follow along as the passage is proclaimed. When everyone is quiet and ready, proclaim John 11:1–44, or if you have asked a student to do so, instruct her or him to begin.

Optional activity: Character assignments
This passage's length and structure lends itself to a dramatic reading involving several people. You may wish to select people in the group to read each of the following parts: narrator, Mary, Martha, the disciples, Jesus, and Thomas.

Step 3 — **Initial Reaction (10 minutes)**

Lead a brief discussion using the following questions. If your group is large, break it into small groups of five to eight people for this step.

17

 • Death

Suggest that the group members refer to John 11:1–44 in their Bible, as necessary.
- What word or phrase from the passage stood out as you listened to the reading?
- What questions or feelings does this Scripture passage raise for you?
- What attitude do you find most young people have about death? Is it an attitude of fear? denial? anger? hope? curiosity?

Step 4 **Commentary (5 minutes)**

After the discussion deliver the following commentary in the manner of your choice (see page 12 of the introduction for options):
- This passage from John's Gospel is a wonderful story. It is a story of loss and restoration, of letting go and unexpectedly receiving again. Hidden inside the story is a second story—the story of Jesus, the savior.

  In this passage we hear of sickness and death, of sisters who loved and lost their brother, of sisters who cared for their brother as he fell ill and stayed with him as he died, of sisters who placed their brother's body in the tomb and mourned him. Anyone who has lost someone they love knows the sorrow that Mary and Martha experienced.

  But this story is different. This story does not end with sorrow. The sorrow is only the beginning of this story. Jesus' surprise answer to Martha's profession of faith and to Mary's tears is a miracle. "Take away the stone" [11:39]. "Lazarus, come out" [11:43]. Jesus is life! *That's* the story.

  The Gospel of John is poetic, rich in drama and symbolism; its form is quite different from that of Matthew, Mark, and Luke. In these Gospels, Jesus often teaches about God's Reign through parables. But the Gospel of John focuses on Jesus' relationship with God and his relationship with his followers through miraculous signs. The raising of Lazarus is one of those miraculous signs unique to the Gospel of John—it is not repeated in the other Gospels. This passage reveals Jesus' close relationships with those he loves. It also reveals his intimate relationship with God, who gives him power over death. The story reveals what Martha has proclaimed, "You are the Messiah, the Son of God, the one coming into the world" [11:27].

  Through great irony this story also reveals that life and death are intimately connected. Unbelievably, by raising Lazarus, Jesus signs his own death sentence. Jesus' returning to Judea and raising a man from the dead so stirs the people that the Pharisees and the high priest are worried that the Romans will destroy the Jews. In the verses that directly follow this story, the Pharisees and the high priest decide to arrest and kill Jesus to save the people. Chapter 11 is meant to prepare the reader for chapter 20. The story of Lazarus's death and resurrection is meant to prepare the reader for Jesus' own death and Resurrection.

  John's Gospel was written for a diverse community—Jews, Greeks, and Samaritans. The community of John was also under scrutiny and received criticism from many directions, including from the Pharisees and other Christians whose beliefs differed from theirs. The power of this story must have given the people of John's community strength and hope. It is a story that also gives us strength and hope in knowing that Jesus is the Resurrection and the life. The death of those we love will cause us sadness as the death of Jesus' loved ones caused him sadness. But we also know that death is not the end for those who believe!

Step 5   Application (15-25 minutes)

Use the following questions to involve the participants in further discussion of how John 11:1–44 applies to their life. You may wish to rephrase or add to these questions to tailor them to your group.

- Does it seem strange to you that Jesus waited to go to Lazarus? If you had a friend who was dying, what might keep you from visiting right away?
- Jesus tells his disciples, "Those who walk during the day do not stumble" [11:9]. What do you think he means by this? Name some ways to walk during the day. What are some of the ways people today choose to "walk at night" [11:10]?
- Thomas and the other Apostles expect to be killed along with Jesus when they go back to Judea. If you were Thomas, do you think you would have gone with Jesus? Why or why not? Have you ever believed in anyone or anything so much you were willing to die for them or it?
- It is Jesus' mission to reveal the Father. In turn it is our mission as Jesus' disciples to reveal the Father and the Son. How do you reveal God?
- Martha believes wholeheartedly in Jesus and that her brother will eventually rise again. Do you feel strong in your belief about life after death, or is it hard for you to feel certain about that?
- Why, do you think, does Jesus weep?
- What is the most important part of this story for you?

Death

 # Live It

Ripples (30 minutes)

This activity focuses on the deaths the participants have experienced and how God can and does act in the most difficult times in our life.

Materials Needed
- ☐ newsprint and markers
- ☐ masking tape
- ☐ string
- ☐ pens or pencils
- ☐ index cards, two for each person

Before the Session
- ☐ Title a sheet of newsprint, "Death of," and write under that the following list: parent, sibling, friend, other relative, famous person, acquaintance, someone else. Post the sheet in the room.
- ☐ Write the following questions on a second sheet of newsprint and post it in the room:
  1. What gifts did this person have? What did you learn from him or her? What positive memories do you have of this person?
  2. What have you learned from this person's death? How are you different because of the loss?
- ☐ Create a set of three concentric circles on the floor formed with string or tape, the largest circle being about 6 feet in diameter.

Step 1 *When doing this component as an independent activity.* If you are doing this component as an independent activity, you may want to proclaim John 11:1–44 and share the commentary from step 4 of the Study It component.

Ask the participants to look at the newsprint titled "Death of" and to think of people they knew who have died. Then ask them to choose one person whom they would like to reflect on. Distribute pens or pencils, and index cards. Direct the young people each to write on the blank side of an index card the name of the person they have selected and to draw a symbol representing her or him. The symbol could be something that they remember about the person, like a smile for someone who was happy or a peace sign for someone who was peaceful. Or the symbol could be an object that represents that person, like the hat she or he wore or the chair she or he liked to sit in. Give the participants a few minutes to complete this task.

Direct the young people to write on the lined side of the card responses to the questions you listed on the second sheet of newsprint. Again give the young people a few minutes of quiet to write their responses.

20

Step 2   Explain that the circles on the floor represent the effect that the death of the person on their card has had on their life. Ask the young people to listen to the following descriptions and place their card, symbol side up, in the appropriate ring:
- The outer ring represents people whose death has affected our life a little. Whether or not we knew them well, their death made us pause to consider our own life, the people whom we love, and what death means.
- The middle ring represents people whose death affected us more deeply. Their death may have made us more aware of our faith, or it may have made us more aware of the things in life that are really important. This death may have caused us either to question our beliefs or to embrace them more fervently.
- The center ring represents people whose loss hit at the core of our being. To lose them changed who we are, the way we think about ourselves, and even the way we live. We will be different now that these people have died.

Let the participants take their time placing their card in one of the rings, encouraging them to give careful consideration to their choice.

Step 3   Invite the participants to share with the group the symbol they drew on their index card. To extend the activity, have the young people share their responses to the questions. If your group is large, let the young people do this sharing in small groups of five to seven. If you have time, ask the participants to make up another card and place it in one of the rings.

Summarize the exercise by making the following points in your own words:
- The rings are like the ripples formed when you throw a stone in a pond. The ripples are highest at the point where the stone first strikes the surface. Similarly, the closer contact we have had with a person, the more his or her death can affect us.
- Jesus knows what it is like to lose someone he loves; he knows the pain and loss we feel.
- The circles are also like ripples in time because both Lazarus and Jesus died and rose almost two thousand years ago. Although we didn't experience their lives personally, the ripples continue to spread and touch our lives and the lives of millions of people.

Alternative Approach   **Remember Me**
This alternative approach can replace the Live It component. Ask the participants to design a memorial for someone they know who has died. They should first decide what kind of memorial it would be: a service, a statue, a park, a scholarship, an event, and so on. Once they have decided on the type of memorial, direct them to write or draw specific plans for it.

After they finish lead a discussion with questions like the following:
- Why did you choose this type of memorial?
- How does the memorial reflect the life and legacy of the person who died?
- How would the memorial affect the friends and relatives of this person?

Death

Pray It

Seeds of New Life (15 minutes)

Materials Needed
- ☐ a small table
- ☐ a candle and matches
- ☐ a plastic foam cup filled with potting soil, one for each person
- ☐ Bibles, one for each person
- ☐ seeds, one for each person

Before the Session
- ☐ Set a table in the center of the room where the group will gather, and place on it a candle, matches, and plastic foam cups of potting soil, one for each person.

Prayer Directions

Ask the young people to open their Bible to John 12:24–25. Give each participant a seed. Dim the lights and light the candle. Ask the young people to hold the seed in their hand and to focus on it while you read the following reflection. Read slowly and pause briefly between paragraphs.

- This seed that you hold in your hand was once a part of a living, growing plant. The plant began from another seed. The plant grew and flowered in the miraculous way that all plants do.

  It withered and died, and that appeared to be its end, but here in your hand is a tiny part of that dead plant. This little seed, nothing much to look at now, is a symbol of God's promise of resurrection.

  We know that when we plant this seed, it will come to life again. Like Lazarus placed in his tomb, like the people we love who have died, like each of us at the end of our life, we must die to come into eternal life with God.

  In the Scriptures Jesus says, "Unless a grain of wheat falls into the earth and dies, it remains just a single grain; but if it dies, it bears much fruit" [John 12:24]. So it was with Jesus; he died and came to life again. So it is with us; we will die and rise again. So it is with this little seed.

  This seed will go into darkness, under the soil, and grow toward the warmth and the light until its resurrection is evident to all who see.

  Let this seed be a reminder of Jesus' promise, "I am the resurrection and the life. Those who believe in me, even though they die, will live, and everyone who lives and believes in me will never die" [11:25–26].

  Invite the young people to take a cup, plant their seed, and return to their place. Then read aloud John 12:24–25. Tell the young people to hold their cup in one hand and raise their other hand over it in blessing as you offer this prayer or a similar prayer in your own words:

Death •

- Lord, we ask your blessing on these seeds. Let them remind us of your promise of eternal life. Help us to know that as surely as this seed will come to life again, we will rise to be with you in heaven. Strengthen our faith. Help us always to remember that like Mary and Martha and their brother, Lazarus, the people whom we love are not lost to us, that you, the God of healing and hope and restoration, will bring us together again. We pray in the name of Jesus, the risen Lord. Amen.

Session Follow-Up

Family Connection

Invite the participants to take home their index card or cards and seed cup and share them with their family. Suggest that they ask a parent or the whole family to share favorite memories about a family member or friend who has died.

Daily Reading and Reflection

ScriptureWalk Bookmark

Distribute to the participants the bookmark for this session, found in appendix B. Point out that the bookmark has scriptural passages and questions on it. Invite the young people to deepen their understanding of the scriptural teaching on death and resurrection by reading the passages and reflecting or journaling on the questions over the next several days.

Session 2

Discipleship

Luke 9:1–6 Many Christians don't often think of themselves as disciples. But the very name Christian implies that they are followers, or disciples, of Christ. This session looks at the passage from Luke about the first solo mission of Jesus' closest disciples. This passage is about our mission as well. We are all called to preach, to heal, and to conquer evil, just as they were. We must follow in the footsteps of the Lord and carry on Jesus' mission.

Discipleship

 # Study It

Disciple Do's and Don'ts (45–55 minutes)

Materials Needed
- ☐ Bibles, one for each person
- ☐ newsprint and markers
- ☐ masking tape

Before the Session
- ☐ If you plan to have a student proclaim the Scriptures in step 2, tell him or her ahead of time so that he or she can practice.
- ☐ Decide how you will present the commentary in step 4 (see page 12 of the introduction for options).

Step 1
Opening Activity (10 minutes)
Tell the participants that this session is about Christian discipleship. Ask them to think of Jesus standing in front of them and to imagine themselves as the first disciples. Jesus is about to send them out on their own for the first time to spread his message.

Post a sheet of newsprint and, as a group, make a list of the do's and don'ts that Jesus might give the disciples about their mission. Ask questions like the following:
- What kinds of things would Jesus want you to say and do?
- What kinds of things would Jesus want you to avoid saying or doing?
- What advice might he give you about handling rejection?

Step 2
Proclamation (5 minutes)
Direct the young people to open their Bible to Luke 9:1–6 so that they can follow along as the passage is proclaimed. When everyone is quiet and ready, proclaim Luke 9:1–6, or if you have asked a student to do so, instruct her or him to begin.

Step 3
Initial Reaction (10 minutes)
Lead a brief discussion using the following questions. If your group is large, break it into small groups of five to eight people for this step. Have the group members refer to Luke 9:1–6 in their Bible, as necessary.
- What word or phrase from the passage stood out as you listened to the reading?
- Which instruction from Jesus would be the most difficult for you to imagine doing? Why?
- Do most Christians you know think of themselves as following Jesus in this way? Why or why not?

 Discipleship

Step 4   Commentary (5 minutes)

After the discussion deliver the following commentary in the manner of your choice (see page 12 of the introduction for options):

- Curing diseases, casting out demons, traveling with nothing—this sounds more like a preview for an adventure movie than what Jesus might ask one of us to do as a day's work. Yet this is exactly what Jesus directed his first followers to do to continue his mission. Although life today is different from that in Jesus' time, the essence of his mission remains the same.

    What was Jesus' mission? The people in Jesus' time saw healings and exorcisms as signs of God's presence. In performing these wonders, Jesus and his Apostles were announcing that the Reign of God was close at hand. This was Jesus' central mission, to help people recognize God's loving presence in their midst. As Jesus' disciples—another word for *followers*—Jesus calls us to do the same.

    But following Jesus has some risks. Jesus warned the Twelve that they would be rejected in some places. They had seen Jesus experience the scrutiny of the authorities because of his words and actions. They knew that by fulfilling what Jesus was requesting of them, they were asking for trouble. We should also expect some rejection from those who do not understand our attempts to share Jesus' Good News.

    Jesus told the Twelve not to pack money, extra supplies, or food. He sure was demanding! But he wanted the disciples to focus on their task, not on their own well-being. If they were to be believed (and to believe in themselves), they *had* to trust in God to take care of them. Jesus asks us to place the same trust in God and not to rely solely on our own power and possessions.

    Jesus' attention was beginning to turn toward Jerusalem, the place that he would go to suffer and die. At this point in his ministry, he had had enough conflicts with the authorities to know that he was not going to be able to continue his ministry without persecution. Later he predicted his own death. He began to prepare his followers to carry on his mission without him.

    We are the spiritual descendants of those first disciples. Carrying on Jesus' mission is *our* job now. We must make people aware of God's loving presence by working to conquer evil (casting out demons) and by bringing God's healing to the lives of people around us. And we are to do this without undue concern for our daily needs. We must expect rejection; the world will laugh and call us weak and say we're foolish to believe that we can make a difference. But just as those first disciples helped others become aware of God's presence, so, too, will we as disciples of Jesus.

Step 5 Application (15-25 minutes)

Use the following questions to involve the participants in further discussion of how Luke 9:1–6 applies to their life. You may wish to rephrase or add to these questions to tailor them to your group.

- This passage talks about having power over demons. In Jesus' time demons were the manifestation of the power of evil in the world. What evils do Jesus' disciples need to address today?
- This passage also talks about curing diseases and healing people. In what ways can you bring God's healing—physical or emotional—into the life of someone around you?
- What tasks seem impossible? Why?
- Share a time from the previous week when you acted as a disciple.
- Jesus was preparing the disciples to carry on his ministry after him. Who do you know who truly acts as a disciple? What is it about that person that makes you think of him or her in that way?
- Jesus tells the disciples, "Take nothing for the journey" [Luke 9:3]. Do you feel fully equipped to go out and proclaim the Reign of God? What skills, knowledge, personal characteristics, or strengths do you already have to help you do this? In what areas do you need to grow?

Discipleship

 # Live It

Following in Jesus' Footsteps (15–30 minutes)

This Live It activity focuses on following in Jesus' footsteps and carrying on his mission.

Materials Needed
- ☐ newsprint and colored markers
- ☐ masking tape
- ☐ scissors, one pair for each person
- ☐ paper grocery bags, one for each person

Step 1 *When doing this component as an independent activity.* If you are doing this component independent from the other session components, you may want to begin by proclaiming Luke 9:1–6 and sharing the commentary in step 4 of the Study It component.

Remind the young people that to be a disciple, one must follow in the footsteps of Jesus. The first disciples literally walked from village to village to share the good news of the Reign of God. This passage is all about walking with Jesus and journeying to Jerusalem, being willing to suffer, to lay down our life for others. Invite the participants to brainstorm different ways people can follow Jesus today. Write their responses on a sheet of posted newsprint.

Hand out scissors, paper bags, and colored markers. Direct everyone to cut out a long side (without the fold) from their bag, trace their bare feet (both right and left) on the blank side of the cutout panel, and cut out the paper feet.

Step 2 Ask everyone to decorate their left foot cutout with pictures, words, and symbols that reflect at least three ways they follow in the footsteps of Jesus, the areas of their faith they feel strong in. Offer one or two examples, such as drawing an ear if they are good at listening to others' problems, or drawing a Band-Aid if they help when a friend is hurting emotionally.

Then tell everyone to decorate their right foot cutout with pictures, words, and symbols that reflect at least three areas of discipleship they feel that they need to work on. Again offer some examples, such as drawing a closed mouth if they struggle with speaking openly about their faith, or drawing a question mark if they feel that they lack the faith to live as a disciple. When the young people are finished, have them share the words and symbols on their feet cutouts in small groups of five to eight participants.

Discipleship

Step 3 After a few minutes of discussion, gather the small groups together and summarize the previous exercise with a large-group discussion using the following questions:
- Did you notice any similarities among people's strengths? among their struggles?
- What advice can you offer to help overcome some of the struggles that were shared? What advice would Jesus offer?
- Now that you have heard from other people, would you like to add any words or symbols to your own feet?

Consider posting the footprints in the room where you meet or a nearby hallway as a "Pathway of discipleship."

When doing this component as an independent activity. If you are doing this component as an independent activity, close by saying a short prayer of blessing over the paper feet, thanking God for the participants' strengths and asking for help in their struggles.

Alternative Approach

Disciples Today

Ask the young people each to write a short magazine article about someone they know who is a modern-day disciple, someone who takes on the challenge of living their faith and following in Jesus' footsteps. Tell them that the articles should include answers to the following questions:
- What is this person's name?
- What does he or she do for a living?
- Tell a little bit about his or her family.
- What does this person do that shows he or she is a disciple?
- What led you to choose this person?

Share the stories among the group members and compile them into one magazine. As a group choose a title for your magazine. Have one or two members design a cover. Share your magazine with another group or make copies of it to give to the people profiled in it.

Discipleship

Pray It

Lord, Bless Our Feet (15 minutes)

Materials Needed
- ☐ a small table
- ☐ a small dish of baby oil or olive oil
- ☐ a candle and matches
- ☐ Bibles, one for each person and one for the prayer table
- ☐ copies of handout 2–A, "Lord, Bless Our Feet," one for each person
- ☐ a tape or CD player, and a recording of reflective instrumental music (optional)

Before the Session
- ☐ Prepare a prayer space by placing on a small table a small dish of baby oil or olive oil, a candle and matches, and an open Bible.
- ☐ Choose five people for the reader parts on handout 2–A, "Lord, Bless Our Feet," and give them a few minutes to read over their part.

Prayer Directions

Ask the young people to take off their shoes and to locate Luke 9:1–6 in their Bible. Light the candle. Proclaim Luke 9:1–6.

Explain that throughout the Scriptures, people chosen by God to do special jobs were anointed with oil. Jesus was referred to as the Anointed One. Anointing is used in our sacraments today. Invite the young people to come to the prayer table and have their feet anointed. Explain that you will anoint the first person by making the sign of the cross on the tops of her or his feet. Then that person will stay to anoint the next person to come forward, and so on, until everyone has had her or his feet anointed. After the last participant has come forward and been anointed, ask that person to anoint your feet. You may wish to play a recording of soft, instrumental music during the ceremony.

Close with the prayer on handout 2–A, "Lord, Bless Our Feet," inviting the volunteer readers you selected to begin.

Session Follow-Up

Family Connection

Invite the participants to ask their family to define what it means to be a disciple and whether they see themselves as disciples. Suggest that the young people share Luke 9:1–6 with their family and discuss how they might respond to this commission from Jesus. Invite them to take home handout 2–A to use for a family prayer time.

Discipleship

Daily Reading and Reflection

ScriptureWalk Bookmark
Distribute to the participants the bookmark for this session, found in appendix B. Point out that the bookmark has scriptural passages and questions on it. Invite the young people to deepen their understanding of the scriptural teaching on discipleship by reading the passages and reflecting or journaling on the questions over the next several days.

Lord, Bless Our Feet

Reader 1. Lord, you have called us to serve, to be your disciples, to carry on your mission, to walk in your footsteps. Help us to follow you.

All. Lord, bless our feet.

Reader 2. Lord, you washed your disciples' feet to show them how to serve with humility. Help us to follow you.

All. Lord, bless our feet.

Reader 3. Lord, your own feet were nailed to the cross. Following you is sometimes hard. It means sacrifice; it means laying down our life for others. Help us to follow you.

All. Lord, bless our feet.

Reader 4. Lord you told your disciples to shake the dust off their feet when they encountered those who refused to welcome them. Sometimes we will feel afraid or embarrassed to share your word, and sometimes we will be rejected. Help us to follow you.

All. Lord, bless our feet.

Reader 5. Lord, we ask you to bless our feet to your service, that we may always be clear in our direction, and strong and steady in our steps. Help us to follow you.

All. Lord, bless our feet.

Session 3

Fear

Psalm 91

Fear is a powerful emotion. When we are ruled by fear, our life is diminished, and we are not plausible witnesses to Christ's triumph over sin and death. This session helps the young people recognize that trust in God is necessary to overcome fear and to take away the power that fear can have over us.

Fear

 **Study It**

Fear Versus Trust (45–55 minutes)

Materials Needed
- ☐ newsprint and markers
- ☐ masking tape
- ☐ Bibles, one for each person
- ☐ pens or pencils

Before the Session
- ☐ Create a timeline by drawing a line lengthways on a sheet of newsprint and numbering 1 to 12 at equal intervals along the line. Hang your timeline on a wall.
- ☐ If you plan to have a student proclaim the Scriptures in step 2, tell him or her ahead of time so that he or she can practice.
- ☐ Decide how you will present the commentary in step 4 (see page 12 of the introduction for options).

Step 1 **Opening Activity (10 minutes)**
Comment that this session is about fear and how Christian believers are called to deal with it. Add that the session begins with an activity about what frightened your group members when they were children. Distribute pens or pencils and point out the timeline on the wall, explaining that the numbers represent ages. Share with them a few lighthearted examples of your own childhood fears, such as, "When I was three, I was afraid of getting sucked down the drain in the tub," or "When I was six, I was afraid of the monster under my bed." Write your examples on the timeline next to their corresponding age. Then invite each participant to share a fear out loud, and write it on the timeline. Be sure to keep this activity moving and keep the mood light. Avoid getting too serious or analytical.

Step 2 **Proclamation (5 minutes)**
Direct the young people to open their Bible to Psalm 91 so that they can follow along as the passage is proclaimed. When everyone is quiet and ready, proclaim Psalm 91, or if you have asked a student to do so, instruct him or her to begin.

Step 3 **Initial Reaction (10 minutes)**
Lead a brief discussion using the following questions. If your group is large, break it into small groups of five to eight people for this step. Have the group members refer to Psalm 91 in their Bible, as necessary.
- What is the basic message of this passage?
- Did your parents ever try to ease your childhood fears by telling you that God would protect you?

- What word or phrase from the passage stood out as you listened to the reading?
- How is fear a big factor in young people's lives today?

Step 4 Commentary (5 minutes)

After the discussion deliver the following commentary in the manner of your choice (see page 12 of the introduction for options):

- The psalms are songs that praise God, songs that express sorrow and ask for God's help, songs that teach wisdom, songs used in worship, and songs that tell of God working throughout Israel's history. These purposes form five major categories of psalms: praise, lament, wisdom, worship, and historical. Psalm 91 is a type of lament that speaks about God's salvation and protection.

   During the time when Israel had kings, the Temple was a central place for the people to experience the presence of God. The psalms were used in Temple prayer. In Psalm 91 the author begins by talking about the experience of knowing God's safe presence in the Temple, of living "in the shelter of the Most High" [91:1]. But then the psalmist continues with a series of promises for safety in all areas of life for those who trust in God.

   Today many things can cause us to be afraid—violence, rejection, failure, losing people we love. The promises in Psalm 91 encourage us: God will deliver you; God will cover you; you have nothing to fear. If you make the Lord your dwelling place, if you love God and seek your safety in God, God will be with you and save you. In the face of all the terrors of life, God's faithful ones can walk through unharmed.

   How do we apply the message of this psalm to our life as Christ's disciples? We should first acknowledge that fear is a normal part of life, that we should rightfully be afraid of some things. But—and this is an important but—fear should not rule our life or be the basis for the decisions we make. Letting fear rule our life will lead to cowardly and even sinful choices. So how do we overcome fear?

   We should start by bringing our fears to God in prayer and to the Christian community we belong to. By asking God's help to trust in divine protection, and through the prayers and support of our brothers and sisters in Christ, we will find courage and peace. Perhaps at first you will experience it just in church and within your Christian community, but gradually it will spread to all areas of your life as the psalmist promises: "Those who love me, I will deliver; / I will protect those who know my name" [91:14].

Step 5 Application (15-25 minutes)

Use the following questions to involve the participants in further discussion of how Psalm 91 applies to their life. You may wish to rephrase or add to these questions to tailor them to your group.

- Psalm 91 promises safety for believers. What are the terrors of the night and the arrows that you face?

 • Fear

- God promises to be with us in times of trouble. Have you ever had an experience of God's presence when you were in trouble?
- Is it difficult to believe in God's protection? Explain.
- Why should belief in God help a person deal with fear?
- This psalm uses many different images for safety: a mother bird, a shield, a fortress. What image or analogy would you use to describe God's protection?
- Share an experience from the previous week when you were afraid. Did you ask God for help or safety? If so, how did it change the situation? If not, how might turning to God have changed the situation?

 Live It

Naming Our Monsters (15–30 minutes)

This Live It activity focuses on the fears we have and how trust in God helps us deal with those fears.

Materials Needed
- ☐ newsprint and markers (use washable markers in case they bleed through the paper)
- ☐ masking tape
- ☐ copies of handout 3–A, "Naming Our Monsters," one for every two to four people

Before the Session
- ☐ Cover a wall with enough newsprint to create approximately a 2-by-2-foot section for every two to four people in your group.
- ☐ Create your own monster on a sheet of newsprint using the directions on handout 3–A, "Naming Our Monsters."

Step 1 *When doing this component as an independent activity.* If you are doing this component independent from the other session components, at the beginning of this activity, you may want to proclaim Psalm 91 and share the commentary in step 4 of the Study It component.

Divide the participants into small groups of two to four. Give each group markers and a copy of handout 3–A. Direct everyone to reflect on the things that they fear in their life right now. Offer some suggestions, such as failure, rejection, losing friends, the divorce of their parents, the future, or being in an embarrassing situation. Explain that each group must choose one fear to illustrate as a monster, according to the directions on handout 3–A. They must draw this monster as a group, on the posted newsprint. As an example share the monster that you prepared ahead of time.

Step 2 Have each small group share its monster with the large group. After each small group shares, ask the other participants if they have had similar fears. Allow a few minutes for discussion.

Step 3 Summarize the activity by putting the following points in your own words:
- Trust is the antidote for fear. When we were small children, trust in our parents helped us not be afraid. Trust in God can help us deal with the fears we encounter in our life now.
- Fear can keep us from reaching our potential. As Christians, dealing with our fears is important. Fear can hold us back in our relationships and achievements. Seeking God can move us beyond fear.

 • Fear

- Christ conquered sin and death because of his trust in God. We truly have nothing to fear when we trust in God.

When doing this component as an independent activity. If you are using this component as an independent activity, you can extend it by having the group members brainstorm other situations that cause people their age to be afraid. After listing these situations on newsprint, spend a few minutes discussing the monster characteristics from handout 3–A.

Alternative Approach

Fear-Full

This alternative approach can replace the Live It component. Give everyone a sheet of paper and direct them each to write down one of their fears. Instruct them to crumple the paper and toss it into a bucket. Remove the fears from the bucket one at a time, open them, read aloud the fear, and discuss it with questions like the following:
- Why might someone have this fear?
- What are some positive ways to deal with this fear?

After all the fears have been discussed, pour a bag of candy into the bucket and explain that when we *empty* ourselves of our fears, God can *fill* us with good things! Pass the bucket and share the candy.

Fear

 # Pray It

Releasing Our Fears (15 minutes)

Materials Needed
- ☐ Bibles, one for each person
- ☐ markers, one for each person
- ☐ large, uninflated balloons, one for each person
- ☐ a candle and matches
- ☐ a tape or CD player, and a recording of reflective instrumental music

Prayer Directions

When doing this component as an independent activity. If you are doing this prayer service without first doing the Live It activity, start by having the young people call out the names of things that frighten or disturb them and write these on newsprint. Explain that these are the monsters that keep us from reaching our potential as followers, or disciples, of Jesus.

Ask half the young people to locate Psalm 23 in their Bible and the other half to look up Romans 8:31–39. Give each participant a marker and a large, uninflated balloon. Instruct the young people to blow one big breath into their balloon each time the name of a monster on the newsprint created during the previous activity is read. Explain that once their balloon is inflated, they should hold it (not tie it) closed with one hand and with a marker write a name or symbol of a personal fear on it.

Dim the lights and light a candle, but leave enough light to read by. Explain that each group will read aloud its passage together, slowly, followed by a few minutes of silence to allow the young people to reflect on the passage and the role fear plays in their own life.

Turn on reflective background music. Direct the Psalm 23 group to begin reading. Then allow for a few minutes of silence. If the group is restless, you may shorten the period of silence, but try for at least 2 minutes. Then direct the Romans, chapter 8, group to read. Again allow time for silent reflection after the reading.

To close offer the following prayer:
- God, our shelter, when we encounter fear, help us to trust in you. When the things we are afraid of threaten to overwhelm us, be with us and strengthen us. Help us to remember that nothing can separate us from your love. We make our prayer through Christ, our protector and Lord. Amen.

Have the participants release their balloons as a symbol of trust in God, and encourage them to watch their fears deflate and fly away.

Fear

Session Follow-Up

Family Connection

Invite the participants to read Psalm 91, Psalm 23, or Romans, chapter 8, with their family as a nighttime prayer or before an event that might create fear (a drivers test, an exam, surgery, time apart from one another).

Daily Reading and Reflection

ScriptureWalk Bookmark

Distribute to the participants the bookmark for this session, found in appendix B. Point out that the bookmark has scriptural passages and questions on it. Invite the young people to deepen their understanding of the scriptural teaching on fear and trust in God by reading the passages and reflecting or journaling on the questions over the next several days.

Naming Our Monsters

As a group choose a fear that teenagers experience. Draw a monster on the posted newsprint to represent that fear. Make sure that the monster has teeth and claws. Then follow these directions in writing the monster's characteristics on your drawing. Be prepared to share your monster with the rest of the group.

1. Give the monster a name. Write it on a name tag.

2. What is the heart, or cause, of this fear? Write it on the monster's chest.

3. Describe the monster's bite. That is, what bad things can happen as a result of this fear? Write these bad things on the monster's teeth.

4. Write on the monster's claws the things that help this monster take hold of teenagers. What media messages, cultural forces, and past experiences might give this monster its power?

5. Draw a light source (lamp, sun, lightbulb) near your monster and write on it the things that can scare this monster away. What experiences, relationships, and knowledge can take away this monster's power?

Handout 3–A: Permission to reproduce this handout for session use is granted.

Session 4

Finding Happiness

Luke 12:4–34

Happiness is both elusive and essential. For ages, advice has been given on where and how to find it. This session gives Jesus' advice on the subject. It will help the young people look at their own life: What keeps them from being happy? And how can they seek true happiness?

Finding Happiness

 # Study It

Finding True Happiness (45–55 minutes)

Materials Needed
- ☐ Bibles, one for each person
- ☐ newsprint and markers
- ☐ masking tape
- ☐ small candies (like M&M's, Skittles, or Tootsie Rolls)

Before the Session
- ☐ If you plan to have a student proclaim the Scriptures in step 2, tell him or her ahead of time so that he or she can practice.
- ☐ Decide how you will present the commentary in step 4 (see page 12 of the introduction for options).

Step 1 **Opening Activity (10 minutes)**
Direct the participants to brainstorm a list of fifty things to be happy about. Ask someone to write these on a sheet of posted newsprint. Give a piece of candy to each person who offers a happiness suggestion. If your group is large, you may choose to split into teams and make it a competition to see which team can name fifty things first. If you have time, ask the participants to choose two or three items from the list that give lasting happiness and to cross off two or three that give false or temporary happiness.

Step 2 **Proclamation (5 minutes)**
Direct the young people to open their Bible to Luke 12:4–34 so that they can follow along as the passage is proclaimed. When everyone is quiet and ready, proclaim Luke 12:4–34, or if you have asked a student to do so, instruct him or her to begin.

Step 3 **Initial Reaction (10 minutes)**
Lead a brief discussion using the following questions. If your group is large, break it into small groups of five to eight people for this step. Have the group members refer to Luke 12:4–34 in their Bible, as necessary.
- What is the most important word or phrase from the passage? Why do you think so?
- How does this compare with our society's ideas about finding happiness?
- Do most people you know seek happiness in the ways identified in this passage? Explain.

• Finding Happiness

Step 4 **Commentary (5 minutes)**
After the discussion deliver the following commentary in the manner of your choice (see page 12 of the introduction for options):

- Luke was a Greek-speaking Christian writing in the late first century. Both Matthew and Mark wrote for Christians who were also Jews. Luke wrote particularly for Gentile, or non-Jewish, Christians. Luke's audience was also made up of city dwellers and middle-class citizens.

    One of the major themes of Luke's Gospel is joy. His Gospel begins with the wonderful story of Jesus' birth. Luke's Gospel reveals the tender mercy of Jesus. It paints a portrait of Jesus as the one who is gentle and forgiving, the one who takes pity on the weak and those in need. The Jesus of Luke's Gospel also communicates those same things about God the Father: "Do not be afraid, little flock, for it is your Father's good pleasure to give you the kingdom" [12:32]. Luke sends a clear message: God wants us to be happy!

    Chapter 12 is a series of warnings against the pitfalls that keep us from happiness, the things that might hold us back from the pure joy that God intends for us now and at the end of time. The Gospel of Luke warns about hypocrisy, about denying Jesus, about greed and worry, and about not being ready for the coming of the Lord. Many things can lead us away from happiness.

    Jesus saw these obstacles to happiness in the people of his time and culture. Luke, too, must have seen these characteristics in his community. And these same pitfalls still exist—people still chase after the things that cannot provide true happiness. Jesus' message for the people of his time and for us is to strive for God's Reign, which is the source of true happiness.

    Jesus is not saying that finding true happiness is an easy thing. It takes courage and hard work to go against most of what our culture tells us happiness is all about. Seeking true happiness means putting people over possessions. It means sharing God's love with others over chasing after your own comfort. It means trusting in God over relying only on your own efforts. Hundreds of generations of Christian saints give us witness that true happiness is found in doing just these things. Why settle for the fleeting happiness the world brings when you can go after the lasting happiness that comes from being in union with God's plan for your life?

Step 5 **Application (15-25 minutes)**
Use the following questions to involve the participants in further discussion of how Luke 12:4–34 applies to their life. You may wish to rephrase or add to these questions to tailor them to your group.

- What are you most often unhappy about? Why?
- What do you think Jesus means by "make purses . . . that do not wear out" [verse 33]?
- What do you treasure? Why?
- If someone who doesn't know you looked at the way you spend your time, energy, and money, what conclusions would they come to about what you treasure?

Finding Happiness

- Do you find that you get caught up in the race for possessions rather than the pursuit of holiness? If so, what are the forces that push you in that direction?
- Name a few things you could do to let go of attachments to things of this world.
- What positive models for dealing with greed, consumerism, and distraction from God's ways do you find in your life right now? Which people, activities, and experiences steer you in the right direction, toward true happiness?
- In what ways do you or could you give alms?
- What image would you use for things that wear out if you were explaining the message of this passage to your friends and family?

Finding Happiness

 # Live It

Where Is Your Treasure? (30 minutes)

This Live It activity focuses on the actions, relationships, and experiences that lead to true happiness.

Materials Needed
- ☐ magazines to cut up or wrapping paper
- ☐ several pairs of scissors
- ☐ several bottles of glue or glue sticks
- ☐ shoe boxes or tissue boxes, one for each person
- ☐ yellow construction paper, one sheet for each person
- ☐ markers
- ☐ newsprint (optional)
- ☐ masking tape (optional)

Step 1 *When doing this component as an independent activity.* If you are doing this component independent from the other session components, you may want to proclaim Luke 12:4–34 and share the commentary in step 4 of the Study It component.

Tell the participants they are going to create treasure chests and fill them with the things that bring true happiness. Distribute magazines, scissors, and glue. Give everyone a shoe box or a tissue box, and instruct them each to decorate the outside of their box with pictures and words from magazines. The pictures and words should represent the things, relationships, and actions that lead to true happiness. If time is a concern, distribute wrapping paper rather than magazines with the scissors and glue and tell everyone to wrap their box and print "Treasure chest" on the lid with a marker.

Step 2 Distribute yellow construction paper and instruct the participants each to cut six circles out of their sheet of paper to make gold coins for their treasure chest. Have them write one of each of the following things on a separate coin. You may want to write these coin directions on newsprint and offer an example for each.
- the name of a person you treasure, someone who brings you happiness
- an experience or memory you treasure, or a time, a season, or an event that is important to you
- something you hope for—a goal or a dream you seek
- one way you give alms, offer service, or share what you have with others
- one thing you treasure about your relationship with God or one way you seek the Reign of God
- something you trust God to take care of instead of worrying about

46

Finding Happiness •

Step 3 Invite the participants to choose one of their gold coins to tell the group about. To extend the activity, have the young people share more than one coin. If your group is large, have the young people do this sharing in small groups of five to seven people.

Summarize the activity by making the following points in your own words:
- We are surrounded by many influences that mislead us about true happiness. Our culture, the media, and even friends and family can push us toward seeking happiness in all the wrong places.
- God loves us tenderly and is even more interested in our happiness than we are.
- The things of this world pass away. It is freedom from worrying about those things that makes us free to be happy—to enjoy the life God has for us here and to hope for eternal life.

Encourage the participants to take their treasure chest home and continue to fill it with gold coins on which they have written relationships and experiences that bring them true happiness.

Alternative Approach

Countercultural Commercials

This alternative approach can replace the Live It component. Bring in empty food or household product containers from items such as cereal, hair spray, shampoo, cleanser, and laundry detergent. Have the participants form teams and let each team choose one of the empty containers. Explain that each team must create an advertisement for a fictional product based on the container. The product must promise to bring true, biblically based happiness. The advertisements can be presented as skits, commercials, or simple descriptions of the product.

For example, a product based on a shampoo bottle might be described like this: "Delight shampoo washes away worry, fear, and greed. Use Delight. It will help you serve others and not be attached to your possessions." After all the teams have presented, lead a discussion about how advertising uses promises of happiness to sell products.

Finding Happiness

# Pray It

Leaving Your Burdens Behind (15 minutes)

Materials Needed
- ☐ envelopes, one for each person
- ☐ copies of resource 4–A, "Prayer Walk Instructions," one for each person
- ☐ Bibles, one for each person
- ☐ notebooks, one for each person (optional)
- ☐ pens or pencils (optional)

Before the Session
- ☐ Create an envelope for each participant by following the directions on resource 4–A, "Prayer Walk Instructions."
- ☐ Select a long, straight place for a prayer walk—a long hall, a sidewalk, or a field.

Prayer Directions

Gather the group in the site you have chosen for the prayer walk. Proclaim Luke 12:4–34. Give each participant one of the envelopes that you prepared. Point out the beginning and end of the prayer walk. Explain that after the Scripture passage is proclaimed, each person should open her or his envelope and read slip number 1. The slips in their envelope will direct them through the prayer walk. Encourage everyone to take their time and make the walk a reflective and prayerful experience. If you have a group that struggles with quiet time, you may want to distribute notebooks and pens and direct them to write their responses to each slip.

Wait for the participants at the end of the prayer walk. Quietly invite those who finish early to pray silently for those still making the prayer walk. When all the young people have finished, close by praying the Lord's Prayer together or by proclaiming 1 Corinthians, chapter 13.

Session Follow-Up

Family Connection

Invite the participants to take their treasure chest home and explain its symbolic meaning to their family. Suggest that they ask each member of the family to make a set of gold coins to go in the treasure chest and share them at a mealtime.

Daily Reading and Reflection

Scripture Walk Bookmark
Distribute to the participants the bookmark for this session, found in appendix B. Point out that the bookmark has scriptural passages and questions on it. Invite the young people to deepen their understanding of the scriptural teaching on finding happiness by reading the passages and reflecting or journaling on the questions over the next several days.

Prayer Walk Instructions

Make a copy of this resource for each participant. Cut apart the five numbered sections of each sheet and place all five slips in an envelope. Prepare an envelope in this manner for each member of your group.

---

1 Think about the things that hold you back from finding happiness. Do you tend to focus on the negative things in life, that is, do you focus on what you *don't* have instead of on what you *do* have? Do you seek popularity more than positive relationships? Are you distracted by the need for success or the desire to acquire things? Take a few minutes to imagine all the things that hold you back as links in a chain attached to your ankle with a heavy weight at the end. Stand up. Now make the decision to walk away from it. Set yourself free, walk away from the things weighing you down and keeping you from finding happiness. Take ten steps forward then read slip number 2.

---

2 When you are unhappy, what are you most often unhappy about? What is one thing you can do to improve that situation or relationship? Ask God's help now and resolve to do it! Take ten steps forward and then read slip number 3.

---

3 What are the positive ways that you seek happiness in your life? What positive relationships are you in? What are the things you do that bring lasting happiness? Take a minute to reflect on and thank God for those things. When you finish take fifteen steps forward and read slip number 4.

---

4 What are some of the ways you serve others? How do you help your family? What do you do for your friends? Do you volunteer? Would you like to do more? Spend a few minutes thinking of the ways you can offer service to others. Then take twelve steps forward and read slip number 5.

---

5 Walk forward freely now, remembering the burdens you have left behind. . . . Focus on the treasure that lies ahead. Picture yourself walking toward God's open arms. As you complete your prayer walk, be aware of the feeling of walking away from the things that keep you from being happy and walking toward God, the source of pure joy! When you reach the gathering area at the end, wait in silence for everyone else to finish.

Resource 4–A: Permission to reproduce this resource for session use is granted.

Session 5

Prayer

Matthew 6:5–15

Young people need meaningful experiences of prayer. This session examines the proper attitudes toward prayer and uses the Lord's Prayer to help the participants understand their own style of prayer.

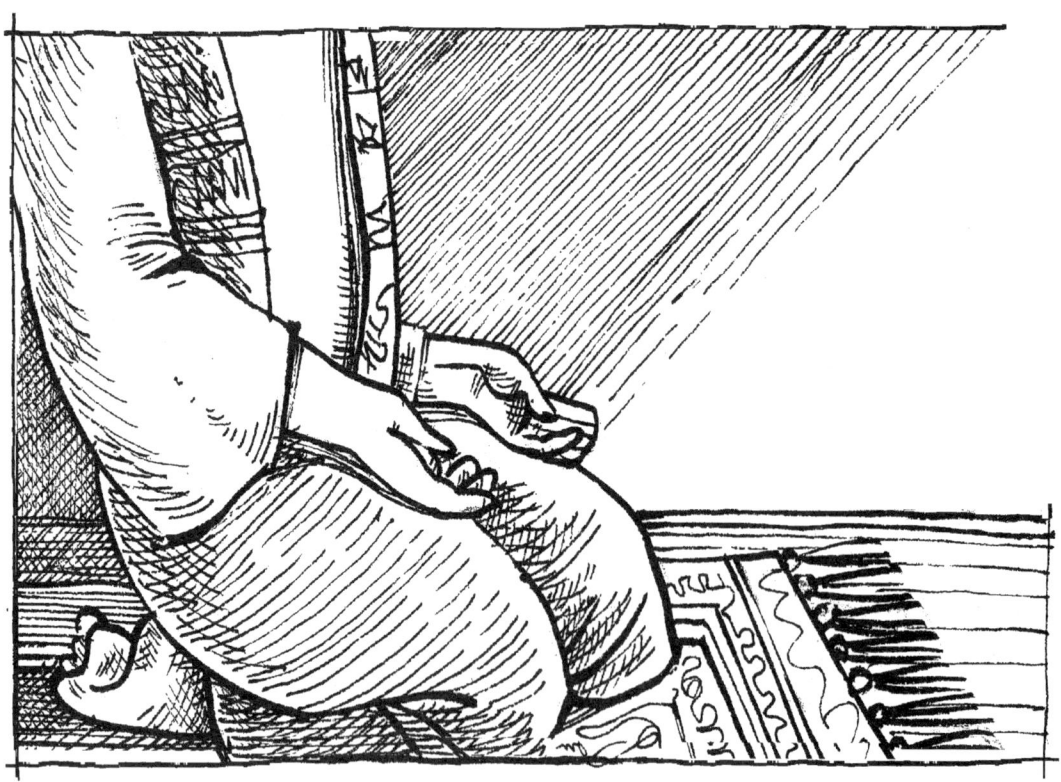

Prayer

 # Study It

What Do You Pray For? (45–55 minutes)

Materials Needed
- ☐ newsprint and a marker
- ☐ masking tape
- ☐ Bibles, one for each person
- ☐ pens or pencils
- ☐ slips of paper, ten for each person
- ☐ a glue stick

Before the Session
- ☐ Prepare a sheet of newsprint by writing the numbers 1 to 10 down the left side and post it on a wall in the meeting room.
- ☐ If you plan to have a student proclaim the Scriptures in step 2, tell him or her ahead of time so that he or she can practice.

Step 1 ### Opening Activity (10 minutes)
As the participants arrive, give them each a pen or pencil and ten slips of paper. Ask the young people to write on as many slips as they can a different thing they often pray for or about. They need not complete all ten slips. Let them know that they will be sharing their responses with the group. When everyone is finished, ask them to share their responses. Place all similar responses together (the slips provide a tally system). Determine the ten most popular responses and write each of them on the posted newsprint next to the number that corresponds to its rank, with 1 being the most popular.

Step 2 ### Proclamation (5 minutes)
Invite the participants to consider the group's top 10 list as they listen to the Scripture passage. Direct the young people to open their Bible to Matthew 6:5–15 so that they can follow along as the passage is proclaimed. When everyone is quiet and ready, proclaim Matthew 6:5–15, or if you have asked a student to do so, instruct him or her to begin.

Step 3 ### Initial Reaction (10 minutes)
Lead a brief discussion using the following questions. If your group is large, break it into small groups of five to eight people for this step. Have the group members refer to Matthew 6:5–15 in their Bible, as necessary.
- What word or phrase from the passage stood out to you?
- Why is this a message that people today need to hear?
- Do you think most people know how to pray well? Why or why not?

 • Prayer

Step 4 **Commentary (5 minutes)**

After the discussion deliver the following commentary in the manner of your choice (see page 12 of the introduction for options):

- In Matthew's Gospel the teachings and sayings of Jesus are organized into five speeches. This passage is part of the first speech, the Sermon on the Mount. The Sermon on the Mount includes many different teachings on how a believer ought to live: handling your anger, loving your enemies, not judging others, and living by the Golden Rule. This section on prayer gives Jesus' followers a model for their own prayer.

  The passage that we read today opens with a warning against hypocrisy. Like a parent who treats the children well when others are watching and ignores them the rest of the time, we are not to be public prayers and private atheists. We are not supposed to seek the approval of others through prayer but truly to seek God in our prayer.

  The teaching in Matthew 6:7 is a warning not to let prayer become routine and meaningless. The Jewish culture of Jesus' time was steeped in prayer. Jewish Law required prayers for morning and evening, before and after meals, as well as other daily prayers. Prayer was nearly as common as conversation. The hazard in this kind of devotion to prayer is that prayer can become just a recited, empty formula. Jesus reminds his followers that prayer doesn't need to be long and fancy to be pleasing to God. Jesus calls his followers to a prayer that is heartfelt, honest communication with God, the loving listener.

  The Lord's Prayer is a simple way for believers to express belief and trust in God. Jesus offers us a short, power-packed prayer that teaches us the fundamental attitudes we should bring to all our prayer. An easy way to remember these attitudes is through the acronym ACTS. The letters stand for the following attitudes that should characterize all our prayer [you may wish to write these out on a sheet of newsprint during or before your presentation]:
  - *Adoration.* In adoration we recognize God's unconditional love for us and praise God's holiness.
  - *Confession.* In confession we acknowledge our own sin and express our sorrow for it. We also express our forgiveness toward those who have hurt or sinned against us.
  - *Thanksgiving.* In thanksgiving we recognize God as the source of all we need, and we express our gratitude for all that we have and all that we are.
  - *Supplication.* Supplication is another word for petition. We ask God for our daily needs and to keep us safe from evil.

  When we make the Lord's Prayer the model for all our prayer, we declare ourselves believers. If we live what we pray, our whole life becomes a living prayer. We do not need lengthy prayer to convince God, nor loud prayer to show others we are faithful. This simple prayer reminds us that God is with us in every moment of every day and that we can rest easy in God's love.

Prayer •

Step 5 **Application (15-25 minutes)**
Use the following questions to involve the participants in further discussion on how Matthew 6:5–15 applies to their life. You may wish to rephrase or add to these questions to tailor them to your group.

- What are the ways that people "pray at the street corners" [6:5] today? Do you think a lot of hypocrisy is present in Christianity now?
- The Lord's Prayer asks God to give us what we need. Is it difficult to believe that God will take care of you? Why or why not?
- Do you know anyone whom you would describe as a prayerful person? If so, who? And why does that description fit her or him?
- In the passage we read today, Jesus says that God knows what we need even before we ask. Is this surprising? Do you feel God's presence in this way?
- Do you ever pray to God from the heart, in your own words? What is that like?
- Do you have a favorite time and place to pray?
- Is your prayer mainly asking God for things? Do you ever just praise and thank God? Do you ever pray for mercy and forgiveness? Do you ever meditate, just sitting quietly in God's presence?
- How could you become better at praying?

Prayer

 # Live It

Prayer Sticks (20–30 minutes)

This Live It activity focuses on the many different experiences of and attitudes toward prayer.

Materials Needed
- ☐ blank paper
- ☐ a marker
- ☐ copies of handout 5–A, "Prayer Sticks," one for each person
- ☐ paper or plastic cups, one for each person
- ☐ stir sticks (coffee stirrers), eighteen for each person
- ☐ several pairs of scissors
- ☐ cellophane tape
- ☐ index cards, five for each small group
- ☐ pens, one for each team
- ☐ game markers, one for each person

Before the Session

Make a game board for each small group by copying the following diagram onto a separate sheet of paper for each small group.

1	Prayer space
2	7
3	6
4	5

Step 1

Divide the group into teams of about five. Give each participant a copy of handout 5–A, "Prayer Sticks," a paper cup, and twenty stir sticks. Tell the young people to cut the handouts along the dotted lines and to tape the back of the left end of each resulting strip to the end of a separate stir stick. Then tell them to wind the strip around the stick so that the words do not show and seal it shut with a small piece of tape. The participants should then place all their sticks into their cup.

Give each team about five index cards, a pen, a game marker for each team member, and one of the paper game boards that you prepared.

54

Step 2   Play begins with each player placing his or her marker on any numbered space. The youngest player chooses a prayer stick from his or her cup, unrolls the strip, reads it out loud, and answers the question. The player then moves the number of spaces written on the space he or she is currently on. Players can move in any direction. Play continues to that person's right.

If a player lands on the spot labeled, "Prayer space," the player must write a prayer intention on an index card. Play continues until the leader calls an end to the game. The winner on each team is the player who is on the highest numbered space at the end of the game. Collect the prayer intention cards to use in the Pray It component. Ask the young people to set aside their sticks and cups for later.

When doing this component as an independent activity. If you are using this component as an independent activity, collect the prayer intentions, offer a short prayer over them, and invite all the participants to remember one another in their prayers for the next week.

Alternative Approach   **Prayer Pretzels**
As a group, make soft pretzels. Find a pretzel recipe and gather the ingredients needed. Have some finished pretzels available to show the participants. Share with the young people the reason for a pretzel's shape: Long ago a monk wanted to reward his students for learning their prayers, so he designed a treat made with bread twisted into the shape of praying hands.

Show your group members a regular pretzel and see if they can identify the shape of praying hands. Then invite the young people to shape their pretzels in a way that represents what prayer means to them.

Prayer

 # Pray It

God-the-Good-Parent Reflection (10 minutes)

Materials Needed
- ☐ a small table
- ☐ a candle and matches
- ☐ the prayer intentions from step 2 of the Live It component
- ☐ a flashlight
- ☐ a tape or CD player, and a recording of reflective instrumental music (optional)

Before the Session
- ☐ Set a small table in the center of where the group will gather and place on it a candle, matches, and the prayer intentions from step 2 of the Live It component.

Prayer Directions

Ask the participants to find a space in the room where they can be alone and undistracted. Set the mood for quiet reflection by darkening the room and lighting the candle. Using a flashlight, read the following script slowly and prayerfully, allowing the participants time to reflect by pausing briefly at the ellipses (. . .). You may wish to play a recording of soft, instrumental music while you are reading the reflection.

- Close your eyes and breathe deeply. . . . Relax. . . . Our Father in heaven . . . God is the good parent. . . . Think of the good parents you know. . . . What words would you use to describe them? . . . Patience? . . . Kindness? . . . Dependability? . . . Strength? . . . Love? . . . Jesus tells us that God's love is like a parent's love. . . . God loves us because we are, simply because we exist. . . . God's love is constant. . . . God does not love us more when we are good and less when we are not. . . . Our successes and failures do not matter except that they may help us see God's love more clearly. . . . Only the creature that God made, you, matters to God. . . . Knowing that God loves you in this way, what do you ask for from God? Take a few minutes now to reflect on what it is you need. . . . [Allow a longer pause here.]

  [Call the participants' attention to the prayer intention cards that you set out on the table. You might invite the young people to offer petitions aloud as well.]

  God, the Scriptures describe you as a loving mother, as a tender father. We place these intentions in your loving hands with confidence in your care for us and our needs. We thank you for the love you have for us. Amen. [You may end here or close the session by praying the Lord's Prayer together.]

Session Follow-Up

Family Connection

Invite the participants to take their prayer sticks home and use them with their family:
- Leave the cup on the kitchen table and invite family members to pick out a prayer stick to discuss whenever they have a few minutes.
- Read a prayer stick instead of the back of the cereal box or the newspaper.
- Keep the prayer sticks cup in a cup holder in the family car for the next few weeks. Have the front seat passenger read a different question each time the family is riding in the car together, and discuss it.

Daily Reading and Reflection

ScriptureWalk Bookmark

Distribute to the participants the bookmark for this session, found in appendix B. Point out that the bookmark has scriptural passages and questions on it. Invite the young people to deepen their understanding of the scriptural teaching on prayer by reading the passages and reflecting or journaling on the questions over the next several days.

Prayer Sticks

Cut along the dotted lines. Tape the left end of each strip to the end of a separate stir stick, wind the strip around the stick, and secure it with a piece of tape.

What is your favorite place to pray? Why?

Is prayer more like a boat or the ocean?

Would you rather pray alone, with a few other people, or as part of a large group?

How often should a person pray?

The most prayerful person I know is _____ because _____.

What kind of prayer do you prefer: reciting memorized prayers like the Lord's Prayer, reading the Scriptures, reflecting silently, or praying spontaneously?

Is prayer more like having a phone conversation, sending an e-mail, or going to visit someone?

If you could change something about the way you pray, what would it be?

On a scale of 1 to 10 (with 10 being very important), how important is prayer to you?

Do you find that you pray mostly for yourself or for others?

Do you think people should pray only for important things?

What is the most powerful experience of prayer you have ever had?

Do you like to pray? Why or why not?

Who taught you how to pray?

Do you find you pray more when you are happy or when you are sad?

What do you find most difficult about prayer?

Define prayer.

My favorite prayer is _____.

Session 6

Sadness and Depression

Job 7:1–11

Sadness or feelings of depression are experienced by most people at some point in their life. For many people such feelings are the result of an occasional bad day or bad week. But for others they are a lifelong struggle. This session uses Job's lament, which gives voice to the sadness and grief life sometimes brings to us. It helps the participants look at ways to deal with sadness or feelings of depression and to remain close to God in difficult times.

Sadness and Depression

 # Study It

Acknowledging Our Sadness (45–55 minutes)

Materials Needed
- ☐ copies of resource 6–A, "That Deflated Feeling," enough of them so that when they are cut apart, you will have a slip for each person
- ☐ a pair of scissors
- ☐ balloons, one for each person
- ☐ string or yarn, enough to cut about a 4-foot length for each person
- ☐ Bibles, one for each person
- ☐ a small prize, such as a piece of candy or a prayer card

Before the Session
- ☐ Cut apart the slips on the photocopy or photocopies of resource 6–A, "That Deflated Feeling." Roll up the slips and stuff one in a balloon for each young person. Blow up the balloons and tie off each one with a length of yarn or string about 4 feet long.
- ☐ If you plan to have a student proclaim the Scriptures in step 2, tell her or him ahead of time so that she or he can practice.
- ☐ Decide how you will present the commentary in step 4 (see page 12 of the introduction for options).

Step 1 **Opening Activity (10 minutes)**
Pass out the balloons that you prepared. Begin by explaining to the participants that this session is about sadness and feelings of depression, then explain the opening game as follows:
- Tie your balloon string to your ankle. When the game begins, try to step on and break other people's balloons while trying to keep yours from getting stomped. Keep your balloon on the ground and do not touch another person.

    Once your balloon is broken, you are out. If possible retrieve the slip of paper that is inside your balloon. Then move to the side of the room and sit down. If the game is too active to get your paper, just sit at the sideline and retrieve it when the game is over.

Call out, "Begin," and let the game go on until only one person has an unpopped balloon. Give that person a prize. Then ask each person to read his or her slip out loud and finish the sentence on it. If your group is large, ask only five or six volunteers to respond. Mention that when sadness enters our life, we can feel deflated—empty and joyless—just like the popped balloons.

Step 2 **Proclamation (5 minutes)**
Introduce the Scripture reading from Job in these or similar words.
- We are going to take some time to study Job, a biblical character who had great reasons to feel sad and depressed. The story begins with a wealthy, happy man who had a wonderful family. Most impor-

Sadness and Depression

tant he was faithful to God. But Job lost nearly everything—his children, his great wealth, even his health. His friends came to mourn his losses with him and talk with him about why he was suffering. But Job was so grief-filled that he and his friends sat silent for seven days and seven nights before they could begin talking. This Scripture passage is part of that exchange.

Direct the young people to open their Bible to Job 7:1–11 so that they can follow along as the passage is proclaimed. When everyone is quiet and ready, proclaim Job 7:1–11, or if you have asked a student to do so, instruct him or her to begin.

Step 3 **Initial Reaction (10 minutes)**
Lead a brief discussion using the following questions. If your group is large, break it into small groups of five to eight people for this step. Have the group members refer to Job 7:1–11 in their Bible, as necessary.
- What word or phrase from the passage stood out as you listened to the reading?
- What line or verse surprised you? Why?
- Job is describing a view that says life is empty, painful, with only death waiting at the end. Have you ever felt like this? When or why?

Step 4 **Commentary (5 minutes)**
After the discussion deliver the following commentary in the manner of your choice (see page 12 of the introduction for options):
- If you lived in Job's time, you would have experienced what is called a shame-and-honor culture. In a shame-and-honor culture, if you were poor or sick, people thought you had fallen out of favor with God. They believed that if bad things happened to you, you were being punished for sins you or your parents had committed; you were shamed. On the other hand, if you were wealthy, people believed God was blessing you for your good deeds; you were honored. It is because of this cultural situation that Job's friends keep accusing him of having sinned or done something wrong. But Job keeps protesting that he did nothing wrong, that he did nothing to deserve this suffering and sadness.

Job's story, all forty-two chapters of it, is an exploration of the age-old question Why does God let bad things happen? It's still a popular question today. The news, magazines, and the Internet are full of stories of people suffering that make us shake our head and ask, "Why?" Some people think these stories are proof that there is no God.

The Book of Job is a rejection of the shame-and-honor notion. Bad things happen to good people. It is not their fault. It is not because God doesn't love them anymore or because God is punishing them. We should take comfort in this biblical teaching. When we are hurt, when we feel sadness or depression, it does not necessarily mean that we have done anything wrong to deserve these feelings.

Job's reaction to his suffering is unusual. Even though he feels sad, even though he expresses his frustration, he remains faithful to God. Job's first response when he gets the bad news is to pray, "The Lord gave, and the Lord has taken away; blessed be the name of the Lord" [1:21]. Job's steadfast faith in God in the midst of his grief can

• Sadness and Depression

strengthen us not to lose our hope either. It is easy to begin doubting God's love when we are feeling sad or depressed.

We should remember that although some depression can be the result of a disappointing experience or profound tragedies like Job's, sometimes it has no apparent cause. Many people experience depression without the influence of any external factors. And some people experience depression that started with an external factor but continues for a very long time. These forms of depression are called clinical or chronic. For many people who have clinical or chronic depression, the best treatment is counseling, medication, or both.

The Book of Job never actually answers the question Why do bad things happen to good people? In chapters 38–41, God responds to Job saying that as the Creator of everything, God's knowledge and purpose are beyond human understanding. The response satisfies Job, and his story has a happy ending—his family and wealth are restored, and God vindicates him in front of his friends.

Job's story is important for us because it reminds us that suffering is not a sign that God is mad at us, and that steadfast faith in God like Job's can help carry us through the worst of times. But that isn't all the Bible has to say about suffering. The New Testament goes further in teaching that suffering can be redemptive, that it can bring healing and even new life. If you want to see a sample of what the New Testament says about suffering, check out the First Letter of Peter sometime.

Step 5 **Application (15-25 minutes)**

Use the following questions to involve the participants in further discussion of how Job 7:1–11 applies to their life. You may wish to rephrase or add to these questions to tailor them to your group.

- In what ways does this passage challenge you? Does it seem wrong to complain to God? Are you afraid to?
- Which of Job's descriptions from the passage was the most powerful to you? Why?
- If you had to describe, in one word, how Job was feeling, what would it be? Think of a time when you felt down. What word would you use to describe how you felt?
- Do you know anyone who has the kind of relationship with God that Job had—that is, a person with a strong faith who can complain to God but remain faithful? Why, do you think, is she or he able to do this?
- What would you do or say if you had lost everything? How would you respond if your friends came to you and said your situation must be your own fault?
- How have you dealt with bad things happening to you? Were you able to keep praying and maintain a relationship with God?
- What would you say to a sad or depressed friend? Who would you talk to if you were feeling like this?
- Do Job's sentiments remind you of a time in your life? Write your own lament or prayer to God about suffering.

Sadness and Depression

 # Live It

Recipes to Cure the Blues (20–30 minutes)

This Live It activity focuses on describing the times in our life when we have felt sad or depressed, and on finding strategies to cope with such feelings.

Materials Needed
- ☐ index cards, two for each person
- ☐ pens or pencils
- ☐ blank paper
- ☐ wooden spoons, one for each small group
- ☐ mixing bowls, one for each small group

Step 1 *When doing this component as an independent activity.* If you are doing this component independent from the other session components, you may want to proclaim Job 7:1–11 and share the commentary from step 4 of the Study It component.

Begin by explaining that suffering is an inevitable, normal part of life. The passage in Job that we have been discussing expresses the extreme emotions that can come along with suffering. Ask the young people to think of the last time they felt sad or depressed. What led them to feel that way? Hand out two index cards and a pen or pencil to each participant. Ask them to write on each card one *positive* thing they do to help fight the blues. Explain that a positive thing is something that doesn't hurt anyone or cause more problems. Their ideas should be no more than one or two sentences. Let the young people know that someone else will be reading their responses.

If you formed small groups for step 3 of the Study It component, have everyone regather with their group members. Designate the person in each group whose birthday is closest to today's date as his or her group's recorder. Give the recorders pieces of paper. Give each group a wooden spoon and a mixing bowl to put its cards into. Explain as follows:
- Each group is to write a recipe for fighting depression using the ingredients placed in the bowl. First the youngest person in your group will stir the cards. Then the oldest person will draw a card and read it aloud. The next oldest person will draw a second card and read it aloud. You may draw a third card if the group thinks it needs another ingredient for its recipe. After you've read your positive ingredients, discuss them and think about how you might creatively concoct a recipe involving them. For example, if the first card says, "I listen to my favorite music," and the second card says, "I call a friend," and the third says, "Go for a walk," the recipe might read as follows:

• Sadness and Depression

> 1 cup of good music
> 1 cup of telephone
> 2 tablespoons of conversation
> a pinch of time alone
> 1 long walk
>
> Stir together telephone, conversation, and time alone. Let sit until relaxed. Pour in music. Mix until smiling. Gently fold in long walk. Bake at 70 degrees (ideal walking temperature) until happy. Serves two.

Have the participants continue creating recipes until the cards are gone or as long as time allows.

Step 2 If you have split into smaller groups, call the groups together and ask each group to read its recipes out loud.

Collect the recipe cards and consider turning them into a cookbook by making copies of the cards, collating the pages, and stapling them together. Give the cookbooks to each member of your group or to other teens going through a difficult time.

Step 3 Summarize the previous exercise by putting the following points in your own words:
- Even though as human beings we are bound to be sad sometimes, we can develop strategies to deal with sadness and let God offer us healing love.
- Research has shown that dwelling on negative thoughts and feelings can lead us from sadness into depression. It's important to express feelings of sadness, but it's just as important to find positive activities to occupy our thoughts and time.
- We all need the support of others to get through sad and difficult times. Brief periods of feeling blue are normal. But when someone feels depressed for more than two weeks and the mood affects their ability to function, they may be suffering from depression and may need the help of a doctor or counselor. Someone who can never remember a happy time, is having difficulty sleeping or seems to sleep all the time, has no energy for normal activities, or has thoughts of death or suicide may be clinically depressed. Clinical depression is not to be confused with simply feeling sad or pessimistic. It is a complex disorder that has a biological or psychological basis and requires treatment by a health-care professional.
- God is present and available to us in our greatest joys and our deepest sorrows. Although we may not understand why pain is a part of life, it helps to know that God loves us throughout all the experiences of our life.

Sadness and Depression

Alternative Approach

Symbols of Sadness

Gather several items that might symbolize sadness to the young people in your group, for example, a hand mirror, a candle, a nail, a chipped or broken plate or mug, a Band-Aid, a roll of tape, a pen, a pencil, a key, a small toy, pebbles. You may want to have several of each item so that more than one participant can choose the same item. Or ask the participants ahead of time to bring in a symbol of a sad time or experience. Set out on a tray or table the items you gathered or that were brought in by the participants.

Ask the group members to think of a time when they felt depressed or sad—it might have been a time when a relationship ended or when they struggled with a problem or when someone close to them died. Invite the group members to look over the collection of items and to choose one to be a symbol of their sadness. Invite those who wish to do so to share with the group why they chose a particular symbol and what it represents. Then lead the young people in talking about positive ways to handle feelings of sadness or depression and how faith in God can help.

Sadness and Depression

Pray It

A Litany of Healing (10 minutes)

Materials Needed
- ☐ copies of handout 6–B, "A Litany of Healing," one for each person
- ☐ Bibles, one for each person
- ☐ a tape or CD player, and a recording of music with the theme of God's love and care for us (some examples: "Be Not Afraid," by Dan Schutte (OCP Publications, 1975, 1978), "You Are Mine," by David Haas (GIA Publications, 1991), "On Eagle's Wings," by Michael Joncas (New Dawn Music, 1979)

Prayer Directions

Begin by proclaiming Job 7:1–11. Then distribute handout 6–B, "A Litany of Healing," and invite the young people to join you in praying the litany. Close by playing a song you have chosen to reflect God's love and care for us, and by inviting the young people to share a sign of peace with one another.

Session Follow-Up

Family Connection

Invite the participants to ask their family how they deal with feelings of sadness or depression and to make a family plan or pact to help one another through sad times. Invite them to take home handout 6–B to pray with their family or to post on the refrigerator. Praying for and with one another can strengthen family bonds and help remind young people moving toward independence that their family is still there for help and support.

Daily Reading and Reflection

ScriptureWalk Bookmark
Distribute to the participants the bookmark for this session, found in appendix B. Point out that the bookmark has scriptural passages and questions on it. Invite the young people to deepen their understanding of the scriptural teaching on sadness and suffering by reading the passages and reflecting or journaling on the questions over the next several days.

66

That Deflated Feeling

Make enough photocopies of this handout so that when they are cut apart as scored, you will have a slip for each participant. Cut apart the photocopy or photocopies along the dotted lines. Roll up the slips of paper and put one in a balloon for each of the young people in your group. Then blow up the balloons and tie off each one with about a 4-foot length of yarn or string.

One thing that always makes me feel sad is . . .

When I feel depressed, I usually respond by . . .

When I start to feel sad, I can make myself feel better by . . .

One thing that always makes me feel sad is . . .

When I feel depressed, I usually respond by . . .

When I start to feel sad, I can make myself feel better by . . .

One thing that always makes me feel sad is . . .

When I feel depressed, I usually respond by . . .

When I start to feel sad, I can make myself feel better by . . .

Resource 6–A: Permission to reproduce this resource for session use is granted.

A Litany of Healing

Leader. When we are tired, Lord . . .

All. Heal us and help us.

Leader. When we are angry, Lord . . .

All. Heal us and help us.

Leader. When we feel all alone, Lord . . .

All. Heal us and help us.

Leader. When we are afraid, Lord . . .

All. Heal us and help us.

Leader. When we have wandered away from you, Lord . . .

All. Heal us and help us.

Leader. When we are without a friend, Lord . . .

All. Heal us and help us.

Leader. When we are sorry, Lord . . .

All. Heal us and help us.

Leader. When we feel unlovable, Lord . . .

All. Heal us and help us.

Leader. When we have lost hope, Lord . . .

All. Heal us and help us.

Leader. When we are in pain, Lord . . .

All. Heal us and help us.

Leader. When we need a fresh start, Lord . . .

All. Heal us and help us.

Leader. When we have done wrong, Lord . . .

All. Heal us and help us.

Leader. When we are suffering, Lord . . .

All. Heal us and help us.

Leader. When we long for you, Lord . . .

All. Heal us and help us.

Session 7

Sexuality

Song of Solomon 2:1–17

We don't usually think of the Bible as a place where we would find a celebration of human sexuality and physical attraction. But the passage from the Song of Solomon that is the focus of this session expresses the essential goodness of our sexuality and recognizes our sexuality as a gift from God.

Sexuality

 # Study It

Sexuality—God's Gift (45–55 minutes)

Materials Needed
- ☐ apples, one for each person
- ☐ Bibles, one for each person

Before the Session
- ☐ If you plan to have a student proclaim the Scriptures in step 2, tell him or her ahead of time so that he or she can practice.
- ☐ Decide how you will present the commentary in step 4 (see p. 12 of the introduction for options).

Step 1 **Opening Activity (10 minutes)**
Hand an apple to each participant. Ask the young people to call out the different things the apple can represent. Then invite them to eat their apple while you mention some other things the apple can represent. Use only the associations in the following list that the participants have not mentioned:
- temptation and sin, Adam and Eve, the apple in the Garden of Eden
- fall harvest, picking apples, apple cider
- teachers, giving an apple to the teacher
- affection, being the apple of your eye
- health, an apple a day keeps the doctor away
- gravity, Isaac Newton, the apple that fell on Newton's head when he discovered gravity

Comment along the following lines:
- The apple can represent something good, like affection, or something bad, like temptation and sin. Our sexuality is the same way. Many times when we talk about sex, it's in a negative way, so much so that we might start to think that sexuality is evil. The passage that we will read today from the Song of Solomon celebrates sexuality as a gift from God to enrich our life and our relationships.

Step 2 **Proclamation (5 minutes)**
Direct the young people to open their Bible to Song of Solomon 2:1–17 so that they can follow along as the passage is proclaimed. When everyone is quiet and ready, proclaim Song of Solomon 2:1–17, or if you have asked a student to do so, instruct him or her to begin.

Step 3 **Initial Reaction (10 minutes)**
Lead a brief discussion using the following questions. If your group is large, break it into small groups of five to eight people for this step. Have the group members refer to Song of Solomon 2:1–17 in their Bible, as necessary.

Sexuality

- What word or phrase from the passage stood out as you listened to the reading?
- Is this a surprising passage in any way?
- Does it seem strange to have love poetry in the Bible? Why or why not?

Step 4 **Commentary (5 minutes)**
After the discussion deliver the following commentary in the manner of your choice (see page 12 of the introduction for options):
- Think about the last time you felt attracted to someone. Did you thank God for the ability to feel those feelings? Did you think of it as a holy time? Have you ever heard a love story and thought, "Wow, that's the same way God feels about us!" Maybe not, but that's what Scripture scholars say about the Song of Solomon, also called the Song of Songs. It is a whole book of the Bible devoted to the love between two people, their attraction to and desire for each other.

  Solomon was a powerful king well known for his goodness and wisdom. Although this book is named after him, it was written long after his death, by an unknown author. The poems may have been a play or songs, or they may have been used at weddings. Scholars are not sure.

  Over the ages scholars have suggested that these descriptions are a metaphor for God's love for humanity, or for Christ's love for the church. Most contemporary scholars agree that we should start our interpretation of the Song of Solomon at the literal level. Its inclusion in the Bible teaches us that sexuality and romantic love are gifts from God, things to be celebrated when used within God's plan.

  This particular passage is similar to the rest of the book in its imagery and style. Here a bride and a bridegroom are speaking. In the rest of the book, friends of the bride, the bride's brothers, and other characters speak. The first section of this passage [2:1–7] is a love duet between the bride and groom, and the second section [2:8–17] is the springtime song of love.

  The imagery in this love poetry may seem strange to us: apples, raisins, doves, and gazelles. The poetry may seem less strange if we consider some of the possible meanings. Raisins and apples are sweet. Today's love songs and poems might compare love to candy or chocolate. The animals represent physical beauty and affection. What metaphors would you use to describe someone you are attracted to?

  The Song of Solomon's last chapter contains a more serious-sounding description of the mystical element of sexuality: "Love is strong as death / passion fierce as the grave" [8:6–7]. The overall revelation of the book is of the goodness of human sexuality, and the beauty of human love.

  When we are attracted to another person, we can and should thank God for those feelings. Inviting God to be a part of those relationships, to bless us and the person to whom we are attracted, brings a whole new aspect to them. Doing so will help us make good decisions with the other person's best interests in mind.

 • Sexuality

Step 5 **Application (15-25 minutes)**

Use the following questions to involve the participants in further discussion of how Song of Solomon 2:1–17 applies to their life. You may wish to rephrase or add to these questions to tailor them to your group.

- How does the message about sexuality in this passage compare with the messages you hear from the media, your family, the church? How is it similar? How is it different?
- Are you surprised to find a book like this in the Bible? Why or why not?
- "My beloved is mine and I am his" [2:16], says the bride. What does it mean to belong to another person in this sense? What are the benefits? What are the costs?
- "Do not stir up or awaken love / until it is ready" [2:7]. This phrase, or refrain, is repeated several times throughout the book. What wisdom does it contain?
- Have you ever thought of romantic love as holy? Why or why not?
- How does thinking of sexuality as holy go against the popular culture's understanding? How do people in love treat each other if they think of sexuality as holy and a gift from God?

Sexuality

 # Live It

Sexuality Pinwheels (20–30 minutes)

This Live It activity focuses on appreciating the gift of our sexuality and considering the kind of relationship that can provide the solid foundation that holy sexual intimacy needs.

Materials Needed
- ☐ copies of handout 7–A, "Sexuality Pinwheel," one for each person
- ☐ blank 8½-by-11-inch sheets of paper, one for each person
- ☐ scissors, a pair for every two or three people
- ☐ pens
- ☐ markers or crayons
- ☐ thumbtacks, one for each person
- ☐ a new, unsharpened pencil with an eraser, one for each person

Before the Session Prepare a sample pinwheel as directed on handout 7–A, "Sexuality Pinwheel." Set out other necessary supplies: scissors, pens, markers or crayons, thumbtacks, pencils.

Step 1 *When doing this component as an independent activity.* If you are doing this component independent from the other session components, you may want to proclaim Song of Solomon 2:1–17 and share the commentary in step 4 of the Study It component.

Distribute to everyone a blank piece of paper and a copy of handout 7–A. Point out the craft supplies that you set out. Tell the young people that they are going to construct pinwheels that reflect their sexuality. Show them the pinwheel you made, refer them to the directions on the handout, and ask them to construct their pinwheel accordingly.

When everyone is done, ask them to share their pinwheels with one another. If your group is large, split into smaller groups of about five to eight for the sharing.

Step 2 Read the following story to the group:
- Once upon a time, a person received a gift. It was a beautiful pinwheel that sparkled in the sun, spun in the breeze, and delighted its owner. It was the kind of gift a person cherishes for a lifetime. It was one of a kind; it was a mystical thing of beauty and power. The person understood that the pinwheel was special and, right from the start, treated it with care and even reverence. Sometimes the person held it up in the wind and sun to spin and sparkle. Other times the person kept it in a safe place to protect it. It was a gift that brought joy, and its owner delighted in it for a lifetime.

    Another person received a pinwheel equal in beauty to the first. It sparkled in the sun and spun in the breeze, but for some reason, this person didn't understand the exceptional beauty and power of

73

 Sexuality

the gift. The person didn't think much about it and didn't consider it a thing to be treated with care or reverence. Before long the pinwheel was tossed in a corner and crushed by the everyday things in this person's life. It was lost and broken and no longer could be used properly.

The same giver had given both gifts. The first person's delight was reflected to the giver, as was the second person's loss. The giver was glad for the first and sorry for the second.

Now one day the second person saw the first with the pinwheel and asked, "What's that?"

"A pinwheel. I received it as a gift, and I've loved it all my life! Isn't it beautiful?" the first person replied.

"Yes," said the second person with a hint of regret and a touch of longing.

The second person ran back home and searched under the everyday things of life until the pinwheel was found. The second person took it and went quickly to the giver.

"I think I've ruined it!"

"Oh, I don't think so," said the giver, "let me see."

And the giver took the pinwheel and made it new again.

The person saw that it was a beautiful pinwheel that sparkled in the sun, spun in the breeze, and delighted its owner. It was the kind of gift a person cherishes for a lifetime. It was one of a kind; it was a mystical thing of beauty and power. The person understood that it was special and started treating it with care and even reverence. Sometimes the person held it up in the wind and sun to spin and sparkle. Other times the person kept it in a safe place to protect it. It was a gift that brought joy, and its owner delighted in it for a lifetime.

Step 3 Lead a discussion of the following questions, or let the young people journal on them privately, or let them spend a few minutes in silence reflecting on each one:
- How are the pinwheels in the story similar to the gift of sexuality?
- Did you identify with either character? Why or why not?

Alternative Approach

Apple Prints

Slice an apple in half across the middle (not from the stem down). Show the participants the five-pointed star formed by the seeds. Using the apple halves and poster paints, invite the young people to make creative prints of the star shapes on pieces of poster board. Each participant should make his or her own creative print. Then using the acronym APPLE, which is explained in the five points that follow, give a talk or lead a discussion on sexuality:
- Accept your sexuality as God's gift. Remember that your sexuality is a good and wonderful thing, a gift to be treasured and treated with respect.

- Prepare yourself for sexual decision making. Think about how you would handle situations that might challenge your sexual decisions. What would you say or do to remain true to God's purpose for sexuality?
- Pray about sexuality and relationships. Let God into your relationships. Ask God's blessing on your relationships, and consider your faith whenever you make sexual decisions.
- Limit yourself. Don't count on the other person in the relationship to set sexual limits. Decide for yourself and be responsible to yourself for your decisions.
- Expect others to respect your sexuality and your sexual decisions. Don't settle for less.

Have the young people take their apple prints home and hang them on their wall or in their locker as a reminder of how the five points in the apple can help us cherish the gift of our sexuality.

Sexuality

Pray It

God's Love Song (10 minutes)

Materials Needed

- ☐ Bibles, one for each person
- ☐ a tape or CD player, and a recording of a popular love song, the words of which could also be understood to refer to God's love for us
- ☐ the pinwheels made in the Live It component
- ☐ an apple

Prayer Directions

Gather everyone in a circle and ask them to be seated. Tell the young people that the recording they are about to listen to is usually understood as a love song from one lover to another. Proclaim Song of Solomon 2:1–17. Then invite the young people to listen to the song you have chosen as if it were God singing the song to them.

When the song is finished, invite the young people to look at their pinwheels and to reflect silently on the relationships they are in now and the relationships they hope to have in the future. After a minute or so of reflection time, call everyone's attention back and explain that you will pass an apple around the circle, and that when it comes to them, they may offer a prayer out loud or in silence to thank God for their relationships, for God's love for them, or to ask God's help. When the apple has gone all the way around the circle, close by proclaiming Song of Solomon 8:6–7.

Session Follow-Up

Family Connection

Have copies of the story from step 2 of the Live It component available for the young people to take home and share with their parents. Invite them to share with their parents their insights on the story and the discussion, as well as their pinwheels.

Daily Reading and Reflection

ScriptureWalk Bookmark

Distribute to the participants the bookmark for this session, found in appendix B. Point out that the bookmark has scriptural passages and questions on it. Invite the young people to deepen their understanding of the scriptural teaching on sexuality by reading the passages and reflecting or journaling on the questions over the next several days.

76

Sexuality Pinwheel

Cut an 8½-by-8½-inch square from a blank sheet of paper. Color it with markers or crayons, following the directions on the diagram below. You may want to refer to the following color chart, which lists feelings commonly associated with some colors. Or choose your own meanings for the colors you want to use.

- red: loving, faithful, romantic
- orange: energetic, active
- yellow: quiet, good listener
- green: artistic, has a strong faith
- blue: peaceful, sympathetic
- purple: confident, emotionally strong

After you color your square, cut a diagonal line from each corner about halfway to the center, as indicated by the dotted lines on the diagram below. Note which corners are marked with *X*'s on the diagram, and bend the corresponding corners or your colored square to the center. Tack them to the eraser of a pencil.

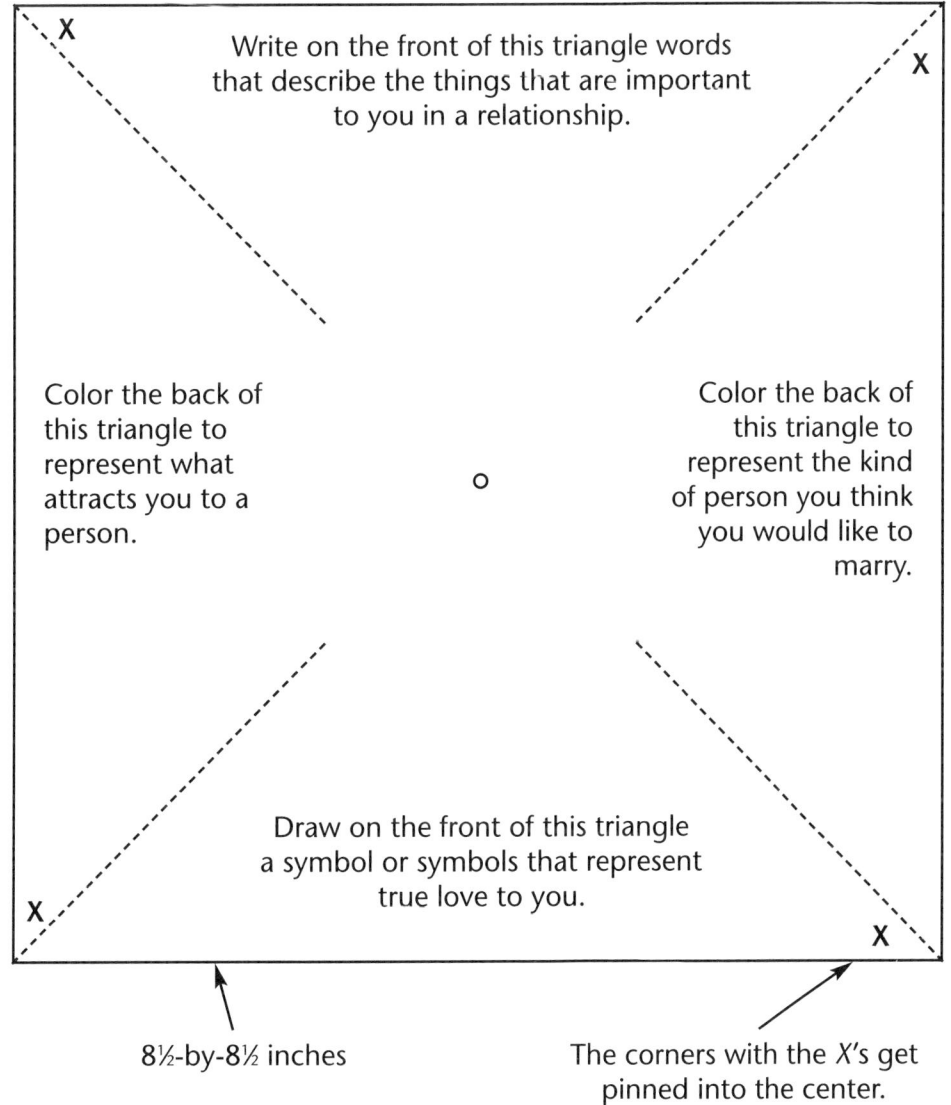

8½-by-8½ inches

The corners with the *X*'s get pinned into the center.

Handout 7–A: Permission to reproduce this handout for session use is granted.

Session 8

Witnessing Your Faith

John 4:1–42

Many Catholic Christians are uncomfortable with the idea of witnessing for Christ. It is not part of their experience to share their faith in such an open way. This session explores Jesus' encounter with the Samaritan woman at the well as our model for witnessing to our belief in Jesus. She, like many of us, had little experience as a witness for faith but became a powerful witness for the Messiah.

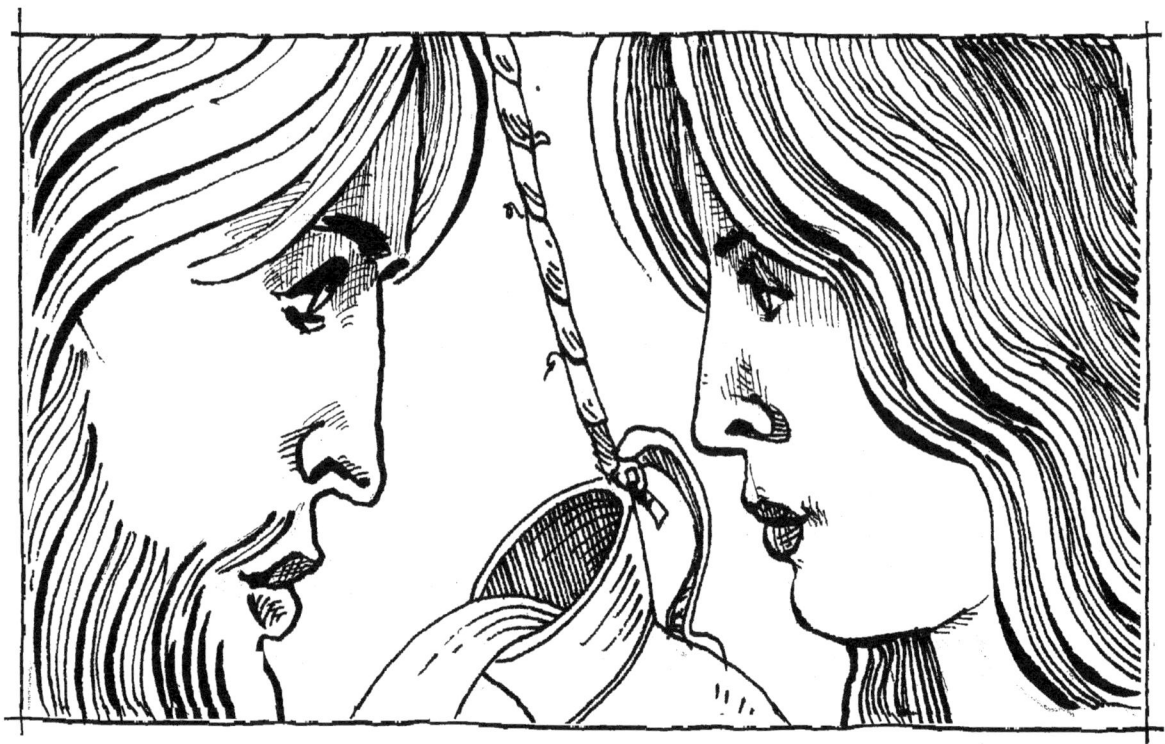

Witnessing Your Faith

 # Study It

Witnessing Your Faith (45–55 minutes)

Materials Needed
- ☐ Bibles, one for each person
- ☐ pens or pencils
- ☐ blank notepaper
- ☐ a milk crate or plastic or wooden box sturdy enough to stand on

Before the Session
- ☐ If you plan to have a student or students proclaim the Scriptures in step 2, tell them ahead of time so that they can practice.
- ☐ Decide how you will present the commentary in step 4 (see page 12 of the introduction for options).

Step 1 **Opening Activity (10 minutes)**

Explain to the participants that this session is about witnessing to our faith. Tell them that they will have a chance to witness to, or speak about, something they feel strongly about, much as the women in the suffrage movement did in the late 1800s. Tell them that when the organizers of that movement wanted to get the word out about the importance of women obtaining the right to vote, they sent out speakers to give speeches on street corners. The speakers stood on boxes to be seen by passersby and shouted to be heard above the crowds and the noise of the street.

Invite the young people to think of something they feel so strongly about that they could give a speech on a street corner about it. Pass out pens or pencils and a couple pieces of paper to each person. Instruct the participants to write a few of the major points that they would shout out as people passed by. Explain that they will have only a minute to speak, so their points should be strong and brief.

After 2 or 3 minutes, invite anyone who wants to, to stand on a milk crate or sturdy box and give her or his street corner speech. If participants are reluctant to stand on the box, let them deliver their points standing up amid the group, but keep the box up front as a reminder.

Step 2 **Proclamation (5 minutes)**

Invite the young people to think of their own experiences of Jesus as they listen to this encounter between Jesus and a Samaritan woman. Direct the young people to open their Bible to John 4:1–42 so that they can follow along as the passage is proclaimed. When everyone is quiet and ready, proclaim John 4:1–42, or if you have asked a student to do so, instruct him or her to begin.

• Witnessing Your Faith

Optional activity: Character assignments
This passage's length and structure lends itself to a dramatic reading involving several people. You may wish to select people in the group to read each of the following parts: narrator, Jesus, the Samaritan woman, the disciples, and the townspeople.

Step 3   Initial Reaction (10 minutes)

Lead a brief discussion using the following questions. If your group is large, break it into small groups of five to eight people for this step. Have the group members refer to John 4:1–42 in their Bible, as necessary.
- What word or phrase from the passage stood out as you listened to the reading?
- What surprised you in this passage? Why would the disciples find it so disturbing that Jesus was speaking with a woman?
- Would anyone you know go around town telling stories like the Samaritan woman did if they met someone who told them about their past? Would you?

Step 4   Commentary (5 minutes)

After the discussion deliver the following commentary in the manner of your choice (see page 12 of the introduction for options):
- Water equals life. In developed countries we often take plentiful water for granted, but in many places pure, drinkable water is a scarce and valuable resource. This was true in Jesus' land and time too. To understand the importance of water in this story, we must step into the shoes of the woman walking to the well.

  She has to go to the well every day. She must get water for drinking, washing, and cooking for herself and her family. Usually, the women in the town went to the well early in the day, before it got too hot. Because she went to the well at the hottest part of the day, we can surmise that she was probably an outcast and went to get water when no one would be around.

  The woman may have been annoyed to find Jesus at the well, expecting him to give her a hard time. Samaritans and Jews were old enemies. The Jews of Jesus' time looked down on Samaritans because of their religious practices. Remember the story of the good Samaritan? That story was a surprise for Jesus' Jewish listeners because in their eyes it wasn't possible for a Samaritan to be good.

  Jesus talks to the woman about "living water." The woman is interested in what he has to say. She questions him. This story further explains an idea introduced earlier in this Gospel. In chapter 2 Jesus changes water into wine at the wedding feast at Cana. In chapter 3 Jesus tells the Pharisee Nicodemus that no one can enter the Kingdom of God unless they are born of water and Spirit. Jesus is the life-giving water. Water equals life.

  Jesus' knowledge of the woman's past shows her that the man she is speaking with is no ordinary man. She recognizes him as a

Witnessing Your Faith

prophet, and Jesus confesses to her that he is the Messiah, the one they have been waiting for.

One of the major themes of John's Gospel is the Paraclete, the Holy Spirit. It is the Spirit who gives us strength and courage to speak about our faith in Jesus. The Samaritan woman's testimony is so spirit-filled that many of the people in the town come to hear Jesus. It is not her popularity that convinces people to come and hear Jesus, but the power of her story. Scholars believe that John's community included Samaritans, so this story affirmed the importance of listening to the testimony of Samaritan converts.

When the disciples return, they are astonished to find Jesus talking with this woman. Speaking with a woman, especially a Samaritan woman, in public was not customary. This is one of several examples in the Gospels where Jesus rejects cultural stereotypes in order to emphasize the dignity of all people. Because of her encounter with Jesus, the Samaritan woman becomes the first missionary in John's Gospel! And she does this in spite of the cultural stereotypes against her.

This story teaches that our relationship with Jesus, the living water, should enliven us, excite us, make us enthusiastic about sharing Jesus with others. It also teaches that no matter who you are, or what you may have done in your life, God accepts you and loves you. Finally, it teaches that the people who we witness to do not have to be far away, in some other country, but those closest to us. Our own caring and loving actions will give us opportunities to share about the love of Jesus that empowers us.

Step 5 Application (15-25 minutes)

Use the following questions to involve the participants in further discussion of how John 4:1–42 applies to their life. You may wish to rephrase or add to these questions to tailor them to your group.

- What if you met Jesus at your local fast-food place? What do you think he might say to you? What would you ask him?
- The woman at the well had a powerful personal encounter that caused her to believe. Why do you believe in Jesus?
- The Samaritan woman was an outcast, but she was still able to share the good news that the Messiah had come. Share a time when you felt like an outcast but still had the ability to do good.
- The author of this passage included this story to give a community under fire the courage to be strong in its faith and share the Good News with others. What story would you tell to other teenagers to help them share their faith more openly?
- Why is it important for us to witness our faith? Why can't we just leave it up to the leaders of the church?
- What are the things that keep you from sharing your faith? What are some things you can do to overcome those obstacles?

Witnessing Your Faith

 # Live It

Telling Your Story (20–30 minutes)

This Live It activity focuses on developing and sharing each person's own witness story.

Materials Needed
- ☐ pens or pencils
- ☐ copies of handout 8–A, "Witnessing to Jesus," one for each person
- ☐ supplies for creating witness stories

Before the Session
- ☐ Choose a method for having the young people give witness to their faith from the list below. Have any needed supplies ready.
  - ☐ a storybook for children—let the participants draw the pictures or cut them out of magazines
  - ☐ a short story
  - ☐ a song or poem
  - ☐ a front page newspaper story
  - ☐ a work of art that illustrates or represents an important part of their own story
- ☐ Prepare your own witness story and be ready to share it with the group. Keep it to 3 to 5 minutes. You may want to use the questions on handout 8–A, "Witnessing to Jesus."

Step 1 *When doing this component as an independent activity.* If you are doing this component as an independent activity, you may want to proclaim John 4:1–42 and share the commentary from step 4 of the Study It component.

Designate one side of the room as "Easy to do" and the other side as "No way" and explain that those two spots are the ends of a continuum reflecting a range of responses. Ask the participants to respond to each of the following ways to witness by moving to the spot along the continuum that expresses their feeling about the statement. Encourage the young people to think about each statement and respond on their own without being influenced by others' responses. When everyone takes a spot along the continuum after each statement, ask volunteers to share why they responded the way they did.

1. I could talk with a friend about why I believe in Jesus.
2. I could visit a nursing home with the youth group.
3. I could write a paper on a religious topic as a school assignment.
4. I could give a faith-sharing talk to a group of younger children.
5. I could talk to my family members about why my faith is important to me.
6. I could put up a poster in my locker with a religious message.
7. I could give a witness talk on a retreat about my relationship with Jesus.

Witnessing Your Faith

8. I could choose a profession or vocation that is obviously religious, for example, a priest, a lay minister, a member of a religious order.
9. I could wear a T-shirt with a religious message to the mall or to school.
10. I could write an article for the school or local newspaper about my church or youth group.

Step 2 Tell the witness story that you prepared ahead of time, modeling for the young people how to share such a story.

Pass out pens or pencils, and copies of handout 8–A to the young people. Explain that they should use the handout to get in touch with how their relationship with Jesus has grown and developed. Suggest that they begin by trying to answer at least five of the statements or questions on the handout. Then, using their answers from the handout, they should construct their own witness story using the method you chose before the session. Set out the necessary supplies.

Step 3 Have the participants share their witness stories with one another. If your group is large, break it into smaller groups of five to seven to do this. Before the sharing begins, emphasize the importance of being respectful of each person's story. God calls us each in different ways; it is important that we respect that and affirm others' witnessing.

After the young people have shared their witness stories, tell them that other Christians often practice their witness stories like this so that if they have the opportunity to share about Christ, they have had some practice doing so. Catholics should be prepared to share about their faith, too. If you are prepared and if you look for opportunities to witness, you might be surprised at how many such moments come your way!

Alternative Approach

The Woman at the Movies
This alternative approach can replace the Live It component. Have the group write the story of the woman at the well in a modern setting as a short play or skit. The encounter between Jesus might happen at the mall or while waiting in line at the movies. Be sure that the message of the play uses the same themes as the Scripture story. Encourage the young people to keep their Bible open to the story as they write so that they can follow the passage closely. Practice the skit. Then if possible make a video of it to share with children in religion classes.

Witnessing Your Faith

Pray It

Living Water Reflection (20 minutes)

Materials Needed
- copies of handout 8–B, "My Well," one for each person
- cellophane tape
- scissors
- a candle and matches
- a tape or CD player, and a recording of reflective instrumental music
- pens

Before the Session
- Consider whether you want to make the wells from handout 8–B, "My Well," for the students ahead of time or whether you want to let them make their own well during the session.

Prayer Directions

If you made the wells from handout 8–B ahead of time, distribute them now. If not, distribute the handout, cellophane tape, and scissors. Tell the young people to put together their own well by following the directions on the handout. After everyone has been given a well with reflection questions in it or has made such a well themselves, set the mood for quiet reflection by lighting a candle in the center of the group and dimming the lights. Leave enough light for the participants to read by.

Turn on quiet, reflective instrumental music and ask the participants each to select randomly one of the reflections from their well. Invite them to take a few minutes to think about the reflection and, if they choose, to write a few words in response on the back of it. Let them know that whatever they write is for their eyes only—they will not need to share it.

After a few minutes, invite the young people to draw a second reflection from their well and again to take a few minutes to pray and think about it.

As time and your group's attention span allows, repeat this process for the third and fourth reflections. Older groups may be able to handle more reflection time; younger groups or more active groups may need to use just one reflection.

Close by offering this prayer:
- Loving God, you care for us and you call to us. We thank you for your care and ask you to help us hear and respond to your call. We pray in the name of Jesus, your Son and our Lord. Amen.

Invite the young people to return the reflections to their well and take their well home with them to use again.

Session Follow-Up

Family Connection Invite the participants to share their witness story with their family. Send home handout 8–A with them and suggest that they ask each member of the family to complete one or two of the sentences on it.

Daily Reading and Reflection
ScriptureWalk Bookmark
Distribute to the participants the bookmark for this session, found in appendix B. Point out that the bookmark has scriptural passages and questions on it. Invite the young people to deepen their understanding of the scriptural teaching on witnessing to our faith by reading the passages and reflecting or journaling on the questions over the next several days.

Witnessing to Jesus

In the story of the woman at the well, Jesus tells the woman about her past. He offers her eternal life. What has Jesus done for you? Choose at least five of the sentences below to complete. After you have completed them, use them to construct your own witness story.

1. When I was little, _____ taught me about Jesus.
2. _____ taught me to pray.
3. I remember learning about Jesus from _____.
4. My earliest memory of Jesus is _____.
5. A time that I've experienced Jesus recently is _____.
6. When I was little, I would pray by _____.
7. When I pray now, I usually _____.
8. I believe in Jesus because _____.
9. Something Jesus does for me is _____.
10. Something I do for Jesus is _____.
11. One of my favorite stories from the Bible is _____. I like it because _____.
12. When I picture Jesus, I _____.
13. When I think about Jesus, I _____.
14. I am grateful to Jesus because _____.
15. A time I felt really close to Jesus is _____.
16. A time I really needed Jesus was when _____.
17. Jesus has changed my life by _____.
18. To me the most important thing Jesus did or said was _____.
19. I am glad that Jesus lived, died, and rose again because _____.
20. I know Jesus loves me because _____.

Handout 8–A: Permission to reproduce this handout for session use is granted.

My Well

Cut along the dotted lines. Tape together the sides of your well. Fold down the triangles to form the bottom of the well and tape them in place, as illustrated on page 2 of the handout. Place the four reflection sections in the well.

"Jesus said to her, 'Everyone who drinks of this water will be thirsty again, but those who drink of the water that I will give them will never be thirsty. The water that I will give will become in them a spring of water gushing up to eternal life'" (John 4:13–14).

How has Jesus given you water or quenched your thirst? In what ways has God come through for you? Where and when do you see God acting in your life?

"Jesus said to them, 'My food is to do the will of him who sent me and to complete his work'" (John 4:34).

Think of a word, phrase, or picture that could represent God's will in your life.

"But I tell you, look around you, see how the fields are ripe for harvesting" (John 4:35).

In what ways is God calling you to harvest? What opportunities do you have to bring others to Christ? to share your faith? to serve? Think of the names of the people whose lives could be influenced by your example of faith.

"They said to the woman, 'It is no longer because of what you have said that we believe, for we have heard for ourselves, and we know that this is truly the Savior of the world'" (John 4:42).

In what ways have you heard for yourself? How has God moved you beyond the faith that you received originally through someone else (for example, your parents or grandparents) to a faith you can call your own? What experiences and relationships have helped you to hear for yourself?

Handout 8–B: Permission to reproduce this handout for session use is granted.

My Well 2

Top

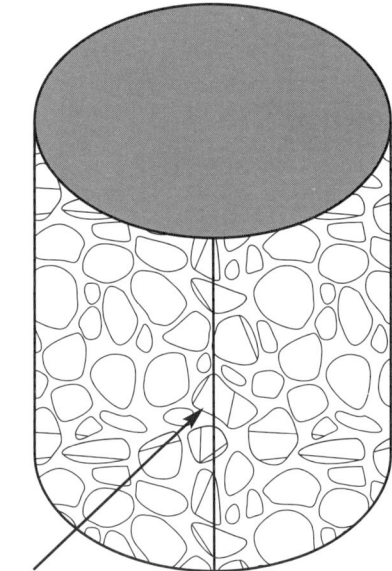

Tape here.

Bottom

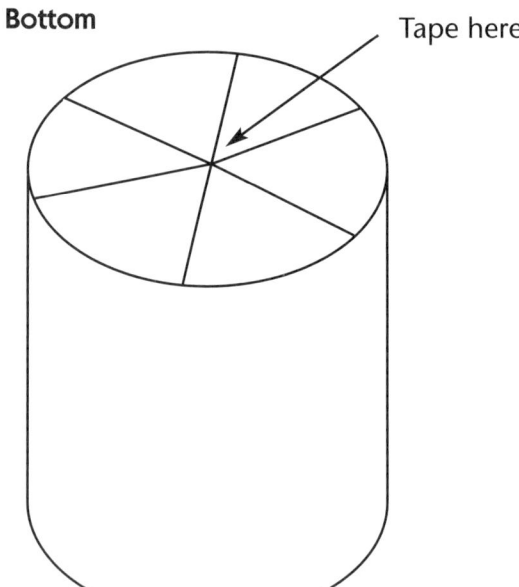

Tape here.

Appendix A

Reading the Scriptures as a Catholic

by Bishop Richard J. Sklba

Like all other Christians, we Catholics bring our faith to everything we do, namely, the basic conviction that Jesus is the risen Lord, who shares his spirit with his disciples through baptism and continues to send us forth to proclaim the Good News. In opening the pages of the Scriptures, we believe that God has chosen a people and guided them through the centuries. As believers, we find biblical witness to all the ways God has loved his people into goodness.

As human beings blessed with intellectual gifts of understanding, imagination, and curiosity, we Catholics, like our Protestant neighbors, also read the Scriptures with eyes, heads, and hearts wide open. We look for everything, somewhat the way a person might read a letter from a distant friend or fiancée, searching for any clue or signal of how things are going.

But besides those attitudes common to most other Christians, there are some special perspectives that we Catholics bring to private Bible study or prayerful use of the Scriptures. Allow me to list a few for the record:

As Catholics we know that the church has placed the Scriptures in our hands. By that I mean that the early Christian community selected those writings believed to be inspired by God. Successive generations carefully monitored the faithful transmission of these works and their translation over the centuries.

On the copyright page, a small cross with the word *imprimatur* and the name of an individual bishop signals the church's formal approval of the faithfulness of the translation we have in hand. Look for it when buying a Bible for someone. It is Catholic to be conscious of the way in which the church takes responsibility for bringing the word to us.

We Catholics pay special attention to the verbs. Perhaps you never thought about it, but the name of Israel's God is a verb, namely, YHWH (probably meaning, "He will make happen" or "he will call into existence"), and indeed the name of Jesus means, "He will save." Moreover, we regularly recite the creed's list of all God's activities—creating, choosing, loving, redeeming, saving, feeding, healing, and so on.

Appendix A

We expect that our Sunday Eucharist will inspire and energize the rest of the week's work. As a people we sense an obligation to open our lives to God's grace, and to be God's living instruments in shaping a more just and generous world. We are people on the move! Granted, we can do nothing without God's grace, but we are inclined toward activity, so we keep checking out the verbs.

We Catholics look for the "us" in everything. Virtually all the books of the Scriptures were intended to be heard and read by an entire community at prayer. We first heard them at Mass. Almost every time the word *you* occurs, it's actually a plural and probably should be translated "you all" in the manner of our southern friends.

Presume that the text is aimed at the entire community, and only afterward see what it might say to the individual reader. In a similar manner, we always pray, "Our Father," even when we're alone, because we have a strong social sense of community.

We Catholics are always mindful of the different ways of saying things. We believe that God chose to take all human speech, except error, in addressing us. Poetry expresses truth differently than a historical account. A proverb is yet another form of telling the truth about human nature.

Catholics, especially since the teachings of Pius XII, are always reminded to be conscious of the larger picture of each unit and are never satisfied with a phrase or sentence taken out of context. We look for the literary "forms" that surround every phase or story.

We Catholics keep looking for the history of things. We know that every biblical concept or practice has an original context within which it was established, and for which it was intended. When circumstances changed, it made a difference. Things developed. Precisely because we have such a constant sense of history, we stand before the Scriptures as if they were a three-paneled mirror in a clothing store, and we see our church community projected repeatedly into past and future ages.

Finally, we Catholics say, "Thank you." We always move from listening to the word of God to a solemn prayer of thanksgiving at the Eucharist, joining our voices to Christ's prayer of thanks and praise to his heavenly Father.

Similarly, every private prayer with the Scriptures should lead us into a prayer of gratitude for all the blessings of life, even those that may seem tough to handle at times. We are grateful people, and we can't stop saying a word of gratitude to the God of our lives.

These are some of the distinctive attitudes we bring to biblical prayer as Catholics. Make them your own, and experience the grace and joy of God's word.

Bishop Sklba is the auxiliary bishop for the Archdiocese of Milwaukee. He has authored several books and articles on the Scriptures and has served on many different committees of the National Conference of Catholic Bishops. He is currently the chair of the ad hoc committee for reviewing Scripture translations.

(This article first appeared in the *Catholic Herald,* 16 December 1999.)

Appendix B

ScriptureWalk Bookmarks

Fear

Day 1: Psalm 27
- Where, when, and why do you seek God?
- Do you call on God when you are afraid? Why or why not?

Day 2: Zephaniah 3:14–20
- "The king of Israel, the Lord, is in your midst; / you shall fear disaster no more" (verse 15). How does this promise make you feel?
- Create a prayer thanking God for being there for you when you were afraid. Remember it the next time you're scared about something.

Day 3: Matthew 14:22–33*
- Do you find yourself, like Peter, trusting God when things are easy but quickly doubting when things get rough?
- What obstacle or challenge do you need to face by taking a step of faith? Take some time to talk to Jesus about it.

Day 4: Mark 4:35–41*
- What storms are going on in your life now? How do they make you feel?
- Remember that Jesus is in the boat with you. Share your feelings with him.

Day 5: Luke 22:54–62
- Have you ever chickened out? For example, have you denied a friendship to keep yourself from being rejected by others?
- Take a moment to forgive yourself and ask forgiveness from God for a time when fear kept you from acting the way you wish you had.

*The readings marked by an asterisk have companion articles in *The Catholic Youth Bible*.

Discipleship

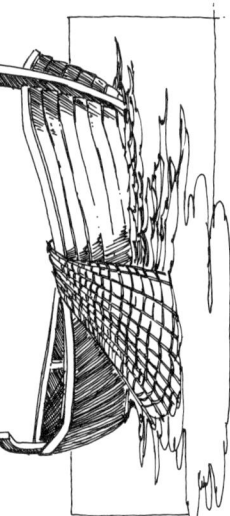

Day 1: Mark 8:34–38*
- To be a disciple means to follow Jesus. In what ways do you follow Jesus? In what ways do you fail to follow Jesus?
- What crosses do you carry? Can you let your suffering strengthen your faith?

Day 2: Acts of the Apostles 4:1–12*
- Peter was filled with the Holy Spirit. Have you ever felt filled with strong faith or conviction?
- Is God calling you to share or defend your faith in Jesus with someone? What can you do to answer that call?

Day 3: Matthew 26:36–45*
- Have you ever "fallen asleep" on a friend and disappointed him or her when he or she needed you? If so, how did you repair the friendship?
- Have you ever let Jesus down? What do you need to do to reunite and reconcile with him?

Day 4: Mark 1:16–20*
- How have you experienced the call to follow Jesus? How far would you go to follow that call?
- In the last week, how have you responded to Jesus' invitation to "fish for people"?

Day 5: Mark 6:30–52*
- Has Jesus ever surprised you with abundance and given you more than you expected?
- What do you have trouble understanding or believing about God? Seek understanding through prayer and the Scriptures.

*The readings marked by an asterisk have companion articles in *The Catholic Youth Bible*.

Death

Day 1: Romans 6:1–23*
- How does the promise of life after death make you feel?
- Is it hard to believe that Christ has conquered death and that our God is stronger than death? Why or why not?

Day 2: 2 Samuel 18:33—19:8*
- Although David's son Absalom had hurt him deeply, David still grieved at his death. How would you respond to the death of someone you love who has also hurt you?
- When have you had to carry on in spite of loss?

Day 3: Luke 8:40–56
- What does this miracle of Jesus' power over death make you feel?
- Is there anything in your life that needs to be healed? Is there anything that has died inside you that Jesus' love can resurrect?

Day 4: Ecclesiastes 3:1–8*
- What does nature teach you about life and death?
- After someone has died, it's hard to believe that joy will ever come again. What message does this passage offer to those who are mourning?

Day 5: Wisdom of Solomon 3:1–9
- Have you lost someone close to you? Picture that person abiding with God in love, and let that picture bring you peace.
- Does verse 1 give you comfort? What else gives you comfort in times of loss?

*The readings marked by an asterisk have companion articles in *The Catholic Youth Bible*.

Sadness and Depression

Day 1: Psalm 22*
- Are you able to praise God when you are sad? Why or why not?
- What role does trust in God play for you in fighting depression and sadness?

Day 2: Matthew 5:1–12*
- What message does this passage offer to those who struggle with sadness?
- How is this message different from what society tells you about sadness?

Day 3: 1 Peter 3:13–18
- Faith in Jesus cannot prevent us from experiencing suffering. But faith in Jesus will help us endure our suffering. Do you agree or disagree?
- Have you ever suffered for doing good?

Day 4: Matthew 27:27–44*
- Have you ever felt like Jesus in this passage?
- Who in your life has helped you when you needed help?

Day 5: Romans 8:18–30*
- What lessons have you learned from the hard times in your life?
- What good can come from suffering?

*The readings marked by an asterisk have companion articles in *The Catholic Youth Bible*.

Prayer

Day 1: Numbers 6:22–27*
- Who would you like to pray this prayer of blessing for?
- When have you heard this blessing before? Think of an occasion to use this blessing—the end of the day, a family event, a trip, a graduation—and pray it!

Day 2: 1 Samuel 2:1–10*
- Hannah's prayer praises God's goodness and strength. What do you praise God for?
- Hannah prayed for a child. What do you ask of God?

Day 3: 1 Samuel 3:1–19*
- When you pray do you spend most of your time talking or listening?
- What steps can you take to better hear God's voice?

Day 4: Psalm 51*
- How do you pray for forgiveness when you're sorry for something you've done?
- How does the sacrament of Reconciliation, part of the church's communal prayer, play a role in your life?

Day 5: Luke 18:1–8*
- What does this passage tell you about prayer?
- In what ways can you add to your prayer life?

*The readings marked by an asterisk have companion articles in *The Catholic Youth Bible*.

Finding Happiness

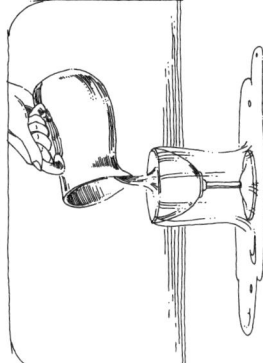

Day 1: Philippians 4:4–9*
- Is *your* gentleness known? Seek peace and strive to be a peaceful person.
- Practice positive thinking. Think of someone you don't get along with, then make a list of all the good things about that person.

Day 2: Genesis 9:8–17*
- What do you think of when you see a rainbow? Does joy fill you up?
- Make a covenant promise with God. Make two columns. In one column write down your promises to God. In the other column write down all the promises God makes to us in the Bible.

Day 3: Sirach 25:1–11
- Why is faithfulness to God the most important part of happiness?
- Harmony among siblings, neighbors, and spouses is highly praised in this passage. Why is it so hard to get along with the people we are closest to?

Day 4: Isaiah 56:1–8*
- What does it mean to "maintain justice" (verse 1)?
- Do you feel like someone who is "joined to the LORD" (verse 3)? If not, what do you need to do to connect yourself to God more?

Day 5: Luke 1:39–56*
- What do you praise God for? When does your soul rejoice in God?
- In what ways have you experienced God's mercy?

*The readings marked by an asterisk have companion articles in *The Catholic Youth Bible*.

Witnessing Your Faith

Day 1: 1 Timothy 4:7–10*
- On a scale of 1 to 10, how would you rate your faithfulness to the teaching of the Bible and the church? Why?
- How can you live out the call of this passage to grow in godliness in your own life?

Day 2: Acts of the Apostles 1:1–11*
- What experiences of Jesus have you had that you can share with others?
- How are you or can you be a witness of Jesus' message?

Day 3: 2 Corinthians 4:5–10*
- How are you light? When and how does the light of Christ shine through you?
- How can you point others toward Jesus without making yourself the center of attention?

Day 4: 2 Timothy 1:3–18*
- Have you ever felt ashamed or embarrassed about your faith?
- Who in your life can serve as an example for you to be strong in sharing faith with others?

Day 5: 2 Timothy 2:22–26*
- How can you share your faith and follow the advice given in this passage?
- Do you fall into the trap of arguing about faith with others? How does being quarrelsome affect a person's ability to be a witness?

*The readings marked by an asterisk have companion articles in *The Catholic Youth Bible*.

Sexuality

Day 1: Genesis 1:26–31
- What message does this passage, particularly verse 27, give about humanity and human sexuality?
- Practice positive thinking. Think of someone of the other sex whom you don't get along with and make a list of all the good things about that person.

Day 2: Tobit 8:4–9
- Tobias and Sarah were devoted to God, to their families, and to each other. Why is such devotion important for two people who are sexually intimate?
- How does love of family and love of God affect your relationships?

Day 3: 1 Corinthians 6:12–20*
- What do you think Saint Paul meant by "your bodies are members of Christ" (verse 15)?
- How can you honor your body as "a temple of the Holy Spirit" (verse 18)?

Day 4: 1 Thessalonians 4:1–8*
- What does it mean for you to control your body in holiness and honor?
- What effect would it have on our culture if people took seriously the command "that no one wrong or exploit" another person sexually? What would change or disappear?

Day 5: Matthew 19:3–9*
- Why is it important for people who are sexually intimate to be married to each other?
- Why do you think Jesus said this?

*The readings marked by an asterisk have companion articles in *The Catholic Youth Bible*.